SPECTRUM®
Critical Thinking For Math
Grade 6

Published by Spectrum®
an imprint of Carson-Dellosa Publishing
Greensboro, NC

Spectrum®
An imprint of Carson-Dellosa Publishing LLC
P.O. Box 35665
Greensboro, NC 27425 USA

ISBN 978-1-4838-3553-2

03-178177811

Table of Contents Grade 6

Table of Contents, continued

Check What You Know

Number Systems and Operations

Identify the property shown.

1. 3(1+5) = 3 + 15   _____

2. (4 + 7) + 6 = 4 + (7 + 6)   _____

3. (14 + 7) · (28 + 9) = (28 + 9) · (14 + 7)   _____

Use the distributive property to multiply.

4. 11 · 39   5. 123 · 21

6. Rewrite the number sentence using subtraction: 47 + 14 = 61

7. Rewrite the number sentence using multiplication: 1417 ÷ 13 = 109

8. Find the least common multiple of 12 and 16.

9. Find the greatest common factor of 48 and 96.

10. 16.35 ÷ 10.9

Lesson 1.1 Applying Number Properties

Number properties allow us to rewrite algebraic expressions in order to solve problems. The **commutative properties** of **addition** and **multiplication** state that the order in which numbers are added or multiplied does not change the value of the sum or product.

$$a + b = b + a \qquad\qquad a \cdot b = b \cdot a$$
$$2 + 3 = 3 + 2 \qquad\qquad 2 \cdot 3 = 3 \cdot 2$$
$$x + 7 = 7 + x \qquad\qquad 3 \cdot x = x \cdot 3$$

The commutative property can be used to help add several numbers using mental math.

$15 + 49 + 52 + 25 + 18 + 11$ can be rewritten as:

$$15 + 25 + 49 + 11 + 52 + 18 =$$

$$40 + 60 + 70$$

$$= 170$$

Complete the equations to reflect the commutative properties.

1. $17 + 34 =$ _____ $+ 17$

2. $j \cdot k =$ _____ $\cdot j$

3. $12 + 63 + 18 + 17 = 12 +$ _____ $+ 17 +$ _____

4. Show how mental math can be used to find this sum: $14 + 28 + 93 + 52 + 36 + 47$

Lesson 1.1 Applying Number Properties

The **associative properties** of addition and multiplication state that the way the addends or factors are grouped doesn't change the value of the sum or product.

$$(a + b) + c = a + (b + c) \qquad (a \cdot b) \cdot c = a \cdot (b \cdot c)$$
$$(2 + 3) + 4 = 2 + (3 + 4) \qquad (2 \cdot 3) \cdot 4 = 2 \cdot (3 \cdot 4)$$
$$x + (7 + 2) = (2 + x) + 7 \qquad (3 \cdot 4) \cdot x = (x \cdot 3) \cdot 4$$

Complete the equations to reflect the associative properties.

1. $(21 \cdot 13) \cdot 24 = 21 \cdot (13 \cdot$ _____ $)$

2. $(w + x) + y =$ _____ $+ (x + y)$

3. $(7 \cdot 1) \cdot$ _____ $= 7 \cdot (1 \cdot 72)$

4. $($ _____ $+ 3) + 15 = 8 + (3 +$ _____ $)$

5. $(10 \cdot$ _____ $) \cdot 2 =$ _____ $\cdot (3 \cdot 2)$

Lesson 1.2 Distributive Property and Multiplication

The **distributive property** is the repeated addition of a sum or difference.

$$a(b + c) = a \cdot b + a \cdot c$$
$$3(2 + 5) = (3 \cdot 2) + (3 \cdot 5) = 6 + 15 = 21$$

$$a(b - c) = a \cdot b - a \cdot c$$
$$3(6 - 2) = (3 \cdot 6) - (3 \cdot 2) =$$
$$18 - 6 = 12$$

The distributive property can be used to find the product of multi-digit factors:

$18 \cdot 6 =$ _____

Rewrite 18: $10 + 8$

Multiply using the distributive property:

$$6(10 + 8) = 6 \cdot 10 + 6 \cdot 8 = 60 + 48 = 108$$
$$18 \cdot 6 = 108$$

Use the distributive property to find each product.

$45 \cdot 5 =$

$37 \cdot 8 =$

$14 \cdot 70 =$

Lesson 1.3 Multiplying with Area Models

You can use an area model to multiply multi-digit numbers. An area model uses the expanded form of each factor to multiply. Write the expanded form of one factor along the top of a rectangle and the other factor along the side. Multiply each section one at a time and find the sum of each row.

$$132 \cdot 45 = \underline{\quad}$$

	×100	×30	×2	
40	4000	1200	80	= 5280
5	500	150	10	= 660
				5,940

```
    132
  x  45
    660
   5280
  5,940
```

Use area models to solve the problems.

Mrs. Harris received a grant for $8,000 to buy calculators for each math student. She needs 96 calculators. Each calculator costs $96. Will Mrs. Harris have enough money to order the calculators? Explain your reasoning.

Mrs. Harris received a $13 discount on each calculator. How much will the total cost of the calculators change? Will she be able to buy the calculators with the grant?

Lesson 1.4 Using Place Value to Divide

Understanding place value can help you use the standard algorithm for division.

$$4704 \div 12$$

```
        392
   12 ) 4704
       -3600
        1104
       -1080
          24
         -24
           0
```

$12 \cdot 300 = 3600$ (the 3 is in the hundreds place)

$12 \cdot 90 = 1080$ (the 9 is in the tens place)

$12 \cdot 2 = 24$ (the 2 is in the ones place)

Identify the error in each problem. Rework the problems correctly.

$1728 \div 54$

```
          320
   54 ) 1728
       -1620
         108
        -108
           0
```

$3636 \div 18$

```
           22
   18 ) 3636
       -3600
          36
         -36
           0
```

Lesson 1.5   Reciprocal Operations

Multiplication and division are reciprocal, or opposite, operations. An opposite operation will "undo" the original operation.

Niki bought 8 pairs of jeans to wear to school. If her mother spent a total of $168, how much did she spend for each pair of jeans? Write two different number sentences that can be used to find the cost of one pair of jeans.

$$168 \div 8 = ? \; ; \; 8 \cdot ? = 168$$

Write two different number sentences that could be used to solve each problem.

Jonathan filled 24 bags with marbles for his younger brother's class. He put 14 marbles in each bag. How many marbles did he give to his brother's class?

Kimberly earned 106,788 points while playing 11 rounds of a video game. What is the average number of points that she earned each game?

Ephraim can text 32 words per minute. How many words could he type if he typed for an entire hour?

Lesson 1.6   Greatest Common Factor

The largest number that is the factor of any set of at least 2 numbers is the **greatest common factor (GCF)**.

To find the greatest common factor of 6, 15, and 21, list the factors of each number.

6: 1, 2, **3**, 6   15: 1, **3**, 5, 15   21: 1, **3**, 7, 21

The greatest common factor is 3.

What is a possible combination of 3 numbers with a GCF of 7?
List multiples of 7: 7, 14, 21, 28, 35, 42, 49, 56, 63, 70, 77, 84, 91, 98, 105

Choose 3 of the listed multiples.

14, **28**, **42** is <u>not</u> a possible combination. Although they all have a common factor of 7, the greatest common factor is 14.

14, **28**, **35** is a possible combination. Although 14 is a common factor for 14 and 28, it is not a factor of 35; therefore 7 is the greatest common factor.

Give 2 sets of numbers that have 6 as the GCF. Explain your answer.

Give 2 sets of numbers that have 11 as the GCF. Explain your answer.

Lesson 1.7   Least Common Multiple

The **least common multiple (LCM)** is the lowest multiple that a set of numbers has in common.

Find the least common multiple of 4, 6, and 9 by listing the multiples of each number until you find the first one that is shared.

4: 4, 8, 12, 16, 20, 24, 28, 32, 36
6: 6, 12, 18, 24, 30, 36
9: 9, 18, 27, 36

The LCM of 4, 6, and 9 is **36**.

What is a possible combination of 3 numbers with a LCM of 60?
List the factors of 60: 1, 2, 3, 4, 5, 6, 10, 12, 15, 20, 30, 60

Choose 3 of the factors:

2, 15, 30 is <u>not</u> a possible combination. Although they all have a common multiple of 60, the least common multiple is 30.

12, 15, 30 is a possible combination. Although 30 is a common multiple of 15 and 30, it is not a multiple of 12; therefore 60 is the least common multiple.

Give 2 sets of numbers that have 100 as the LCM.

Give 2 sets of numbers that have 40 as the LCM.

Lesson 1.8 GCF in the Real World

Mrs. Rankin has a class of 18 boys and 12 girls. How many teams with equal numbers of girls and boys can be made for Field Day?

Mrs. Rankin needs to divide her class into smaller groups, so she needs to find the GCF of the numbers of girls and boys.

12: 1, 2, 3, 4, 6, 12   18: 1, 2, 3, 6, 9, 18

The GCF is 6. Six groups made up of 2 girls and 3 boys can be made for Field Day.

Solve the problems.

Shawn is making treat bags for her friends. She has 24 lollipops, 36 pieces of chocolate candy, and 60 pieces of gum. What is the greatest number of bags she can make if she puts an equal amount of each kind of candy in each treat bag?

Joanie made 8 bedazzled vests in her sewing class for all of her cousins. Give 2 possible combinations of the number of buttons, zippers, and sparkly stickers that she used to make the vests. Explain your reasoning.

Lesson 1.9 LCM in the Real World

Mr. Adams is grilling hot dogs. Hot dog packs have 8 hot dogs. Hot dog bun packs have 10 buns. Mr. Adams wants to have the same number of buns as hot dogs. How many packs of each should he buy?

To solve, find the LCM of 8 and 10.

$$8: 8, 16, 24, 32, 40$$
$$10: 10, 20, 30, 40$$

The LCM of 8 and 10 is 40. Mr. Adams needs to buy 5 packs of hot dogs and 4 packs of hot dog buns so that he can make 40 hot dogs.

Solve the problems. Show your work.

Bob is building a fence with 6-foot sections of fencing. Wendy is building a fence with 8-foot sections of fencing. Leo is building a fence with 4-foot sections. How long are the fences the first time they are the same length?

Three science classes at different schools are studying the growth of plants. The class at Lincoln Middle School measures their plants every 5 days. The class at Hairston Middle School measures their plants every 6 days. The class at Jackson Middle School measures their plants every 9 days. On what day will all three classes measure their plants?

Lesson 1.10 Multiplying Decimals

When multiplying decimals, use the same methods as you do for multiplying multi-digit whole numbers. Consider the place values when determining the final answer.

Sharla paid $4.78 per pound for 2.5 pounds of grapes. How much did she pay in total?

$4.78 \cdot 100$ to make a whole number
$\times 2.5 \cdot 10$ to make a whole number
11.95

She paid $11.95.

$$
\begin{array}{r}
478 \\
\times 25 \\
\hline
2390 \\
9560 \\
\hline
11950
\end{array}
$$

$2390 = 478 \cdot 5$
$9560 = 478 \cdot 20$
$11950 \div 100, \div 10$ to get original place values

Solve the problem. Show your work.

The Robotics Club is buying supplies to build 12 robots. Each robot consists of 1 central processing unit, 6 body parts, and 1 speaker. The central processing unit costs $42.18. The body parts cost $5.79 each and the speaker costs $21.30.

There are 34 members in the Robotics Club, and each paid a $33.25 membership fee. If they use the membership fees to purchase the robots, will they have enough to purchase the 12 robots?

Lesson 1.11 Dividing Decimals

When dividing decimals, use the same methods as you do for dividing multi-digit whole numbers. Consider the place values when determining the final answer.

Jasay is making ribbons to decorate for the school dance. She has a roll of ribbon that is 106.02 inches long. She needs to cut the ribbon into 3.42-inch pieces. How many ribbons will she have?

$3.42 \overline{)106.02}$

Multiply the divisor by 100 to make a whole number. Multiply the dividend by the same number (100).

$$
\begin{array}{r}
31 \\
342 \overline{)10602} \\
-10260 \\
\hline
342 \\
-342 \\
\hline
0
\end{array}
$$

$= 342 \cdot 30$
$= 342 \cdot 1$

Jasay can make 31 ribbons.

Solve the problem. Show your work.

Jeri is making cookies for a bake sale. She needs to figure out how many batches she can make with the ingredients that she already has. The recipe calls for 0.25 cups of sugar. She has 2.75 cups of sugar. The recipe calls for 0.4 teaspoons of oats. She has 2 teaspoons of oats. The recipe also calls for 1.6 cups of flour. She has 9.6 cups of flour. How many batches can she make? Explain your reasoning.

Check What You Learned

Number Systems and Operations

Complete the number sentences to reflect the given property.

1. Distributive property: $7(4 + 6) =$ _____ $+ 42$

2. Associative property: $(12 \cdot$ _____ $) \cdot 15 = 12 \cdot (29 \cdot 15)$

3. Commutative property: $(14 \cdot 11) + (8 \cdot 19) = ($ _____ $\cdot 19) + (14 \cdot$ _____ $)$

Use the distributive property to multiply.

4. $21 \cdot 49$

Solve the problems.

5. The school soccer team has 34 players. Each player will get a special T-shirt to wear on game days. The T-shirts cost $17 each. How much money will the team spend on T-shirts? Use an area model to solve.

6. Lucy can drive 57 miles in an hour. How far can Lucy drive in 4 hours? Write two number sentences to describe the scenario.

Check What You Learned

Number Systems and Operations

7. The new youth basketball league is giving out prizes to recruit new players. Every 12th person who signs up will receive a free basketball. Every 15th person will receive a coupon for $10 off some new basketball shoes. What is the number of the person who will receive both the basketball and the coupon for the shoes?

8. A yard of fabric costs $14.50. How much is 2.3 yards of fabric?

9. Camilla's grandmother lives 23.6 miles away. Her best friend's grandmother lives 3.4 times farther away. How far away does her best friend's grandmother live?

Check What You Know

Multiplying and Dividing Fractions

Solve the problems. Show your work.

1. $\frac{3}{8} \cdot \frac{2}{3}$

2. $6\frac{1}{3} \cdot 6$

3. $2\frac{1}{2} \cdot 3\frac{3}{4}$

4. $12 \div \frac{1}{3}$

5. $\frac{4}{5} \div \frac{3}{10}$

6. $2\frac{1}{3} \div 1\frac{1}{2}$

Check What You Know

Multiplying and Dividing Fractions

Solve the problems. Show your work.

7. Jennifer and Kim ate $\frac{7}{8}$ of a pizza together. Kim ate $\frac{2}{3}$ of that amount. How much of the whole pizza did Kim eat?

8. Anita can swim $1\frac{1}{8}$ meters per second. She swims for $50\frac{1}{4}$ seconds. How many meters did she swim?

Lesson 2.1 Multiplying Fractions and Mixed Numbers

When multiplying mixed numbers, change the mixed numbers into improper fractions before multiplying.

$$1\frac{1}{3} \cdot 1\frac{1}{2} \rightarrow \frac{4}{3} \cdot \frac{3}{2} \rightarrow \frac{12}{6} \rightarrow 2$$

Use the recipe to answer the questions.

Chocolate Chip Cookie Recipe

$2\frac{1}{4}$ cups flour $\frac{3}{4}$ cup butter   1 egg

$\frac{1}{2}$ tsp baking soda $1\frac{1}{4}$ cups sugar $1\frac{3}{4}$ cups chocolate chips

$\frac{1}{2}$ tsp salt   1 tbsp vanilla

Alexis and Dawn are making cookies. They want to be sure that they have enough ingredients.

If Alexis makes $1\frac{3}{4}$ batches and Dawn makes $2\frac{1}{3}$ batches, how much butter will they need all together?

Chocolate chips come in a 2-cup bag. Will 4 bags of chocolate chips be enough?

Alexis and Dawn have 8 cups of flour. Will they have enough?

Lesson 2.2   Dividing Fractions Using a Number Line

You can use a number line to divide fractions.

To solve $2\frac{1}{4} \div \frac{1}{2}$, note where $2\frac{1}{4}$ is on the number line. Starting at 0, count by $\frac{1}{2}$ until you reach $2\frac{1}{4}$. If you can't count by a full $\frac{1}{2}$, determine what fraction of $\frac{1}{2}$ will get you to $2\frac{1}{4}$.

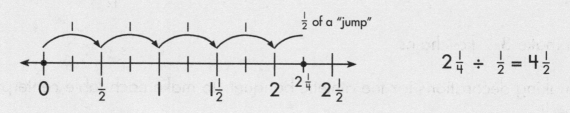

$$2\frac{1}{4} \div \frac{1}{2} = 4\frac{1}{2}$$

Answer the questions. Use a number line to show your answers.

Kim ran $\frac{9}{10}$ of a mile. Adrian ran $\frac{3}{5}$ of a mile. Adrian claims that Kim ran $1\frac{3}{10}$ times farther than him. Kim says that she actually ran $1\frac{1}{2}$ times farther than Adrian. Who is right?

The next day, Kim runs $3\frac{3}{4}$ miles and Adrian runs $1\frac{1}{2}$ miles. Adrian thinks that Kim ran $2\frac{1}{2}$ times farther than him. Kim thinks that she ran $1\frac{1}{4}$ times farther. Who is right?

Lesson 2.3 Dividing Mixed Numbers

You can divide mixed numbers by rewriting them as improper fractions and then multiplying the reciprocal of the divisor.

Sherri needs $5\frac{1}{4}$ inches of yarn to make a braided keychain. She found $16\frac{1}{2}$ inches of yarn in her room. How many keychains can she make?

$$16\frac{1}{2} \div 5\frac{1}{4} \quad \rightarrow \quad \frac{33}{2} \div \frac{21}{4} \quad \rightarrow \quad \frac{33}{2} \cdot \frac{4}{21} \quad \rightarrow \quad \frac{132}{42} = \frac{22}{7} = 3\frac{1}{7}$$

She can make $3\frac{1}{7}$ keychains.

Kevin is making decorations for the athletic banquet. To make each table centerpiece, he will need:

$1\frac{3}{4}$ inches white ribbon $3\frac{2}{5}$ inches red ribbon

$2\frac{1}{8}$ inches blue ribbon $4\frac{1}{4}$ inches green ribbon

Use the information above to solve this problem and the two problems on the next page.

Kevin found some leftover ribbon in a box. Assuming he had enough of the other colors needed, how many centerpieces can be made if he found $6\frac{1}{2}$ inches of white ribbon and $8\frac{1}{8}$ inches of blue ribbon?

Lesson 2.3   Dividing Mixed Numbers

Solve the problems. Show your work.

Kimberly brought some ribbon that she found in the art room. She had $10\frac{5}{8}$ inches of green ribbon and $12\frac{7}{10}$ inches of red ribbon. How does this affect the number of centerpieces that can be made?

Cheryl thought that it would be a good idea to add another color to the centerpiece. She wants to add $2\frac{1}{2}$ inches of yellow ribbon to each centerpiece. She brings $9\frac{1}{4}$ inches of yellow ribbon. How does this affect the number of centerpieces than can be made?

Lesson 2.4 Mixed Numbers in the Real World

Solve the problems. Show your work.

Jim and Steve have started a fence-painting business for the summer. They can paint $3\frac{5}{8}$ feet of a fence in $1\frac{1}{2}$ hours.

1. If Jim and Steve worked for $5\frac{3}{8}$ hours, how many feet of fence did they paint?

2. The Johnsons have a fence that is $22\frac{3}{8}$ feet long. How long will it take for Jim and Steve to paint the fence?

3. Steve got sick and could not help Jim paint the Johnsons' fence. When Jim paints alone, it takes him $1\frac{1}{4}$ hours to paint $1\frac{3}{4}$ feet of fence. How long will it take Jim to paint the fence alone?

Check What You Learned

Multiplying and Dividing Fractions

1. Ahmad has $7\frac{1}{2}$ cups of trail mix. He wants to make $\frac{3}{4}$-cup servings for his friends. How many servings can he make? Use a number line to show your answer.

$\longleftarrow\rule{6cm}{0.4pt}\longrightarrow$

2. Chanel has read $2\frac{3}{4}$ books this summer. Morgan has read $1\frac{1}{4}$ books. Morgan says Chanel has done $2\frac{1}{4}$ times more reading. Chanel says she has only done $2\frac{1}{5}$ times more reading. Who is correct? Use a number line to show your answer.

$\longleftarrow\rule{6cm}{0.4pt}\longrightarrow$

3. The length of a flower bed is $4\frac{1}{4}$ feet. Its width is $2\frac{3}{8}$ feet. What is the area of the flower bed? (Hint: *area = length · width*).

4. Kylie and Connor raked $\frac{5}{8}$ of the yard together. Kylie raked $\frac{2}{3}$ of that amount. How much of the entire yard did Connor rake?

Check What You Learned

Multiplying and Dividing Fractions

5. Jacob drove $15\frac{1}{2}$ miles a day for 6 days in a row. How many miles would he have to drive a day to cover the same distance in $\frac{1}{3}$ the number of days?

6. Marquise has $24\frac{1}{2}$ pounds of dog food. He feeds his dog $1\frac{3}{4}$ pounds twice a day. How many days will he be able to feed his dog before buying more dog food?

7. How many pieces of $\frac{5}{8}$-inch rope can be cut from a $3\frac{3}{4}$ inch rope?

8. Rochelle has $5\frac{2}{5}$ pounds of candy. Monica has $3\frac{2}{3}$ times as much candy. How much candy does she have?

Ratios, Rates, and Percents

1. There are 4 girls for every 7 boys in the swim club. Complete the following table with equivalent ratios:

Girls	4		12	
Boys	7	14		28

2. Lisa found a new recipe for punch. The punch contains 3 cups of pineapple juice for every 4 cups of orange juice. How many cups of orange juice must she use, if she uses 12 cups of pineapple juice?

3. 3 tablespoons of sugar has 144 calories. Sugar has _____ calories per tablespoon.

4. Write $\frac{4}{5}$ as a decimal and a percent.

NAME _____

Check What You Know

Ratios, Rates, and Percents

5. Janet wants to make limeade punch for the party. She found two recipes. One of the recipes calls for 2 cups of lime juice for every 3 cups of water. The other recipe calls for 3 cups of lime juice for every 5 cups of water. Which limeade will have a stronger lime taste?

6. Which is the best buy?

	Size (oz.)	Price ($)
Regular Size Detergent	96	8.64
Family Size Detergent	128	10.24

7. Kenya bought a dress that usually costs $60, but she got a 35% discount. How much did she save?

Lesson 3.1 Comparing Ratios Using Ratio Tables

The table below represents the number of hours passed since Jorge posted a video on social media to raise awareness of endangered animal species in his state. He is tracking how many times the video was watched. How many views were there after 6 hours? After how many hours would there be 160 views?

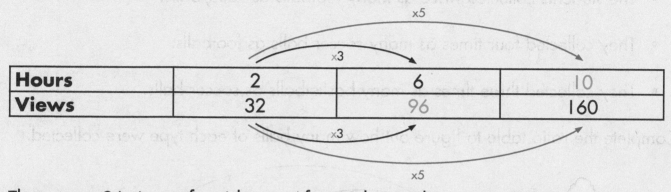

Hours	2	6	10
Views	32	96	160

There were 96 views after 6 hours. After 10 hours, there were 160 views.

Use ratio tables to answer the questions.

A recipe calls for 7 cups of milk for every 21 cups of flour. If Chef Rachel puts in 147 cups of flour, how many cups of milk must she add?

Chef Rachel wants to make a smaller batch of the recipe and use only 1 cup of milk. How many cups of flour will she use?

Lesson 3.2   Ratio Tables in the Real World

Students at Lyons Middle School are doing a service project. They are collecting footballs, basketballs, volleyballs, and soccer balls for local community centers. They have collected a total of 105 balls.

- The students collected twice as many footballs as volleyballs.

- They collected four times as many soccer balls as footballs.

- They collected three times as many basketballs as soccer balls.

Complete the ratio table to figure out how many balls of each type were collected.

x ____   x ____

Volleyballs	1		
Footballs	2		
Soccer Balls	8		
Basketballs	24		
Total	35		105

The students collected

_____ volleyballs   _____ footballs

_____ soccer balls   _____ basketballs

Lesson 3.3   Comparing Ratios Using Unit Rates

Unit rates are useful when trying to compare two or more proportional relationships.

Sasha read 20 pages in 10 minutes. Brian read 12 pages in 4 minutes. Who read faster? How long would it take Brian to read a 104-page book?

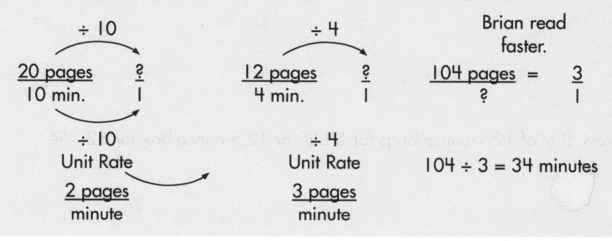

Solve the problems below and on the next page. Show your work.

Rochelle is shopping. She wants to get the best prices. Determine the better deals for Rochelle.

Apples: Single apples for $1.79/pound or a 3-pound bag of apples for $4.89?

Lesson 3.3   Comparing Ratios Using Unit Rates

Cereal: 32-ounce box for $4.80 or 26-ounce box for $3.90?

Crackers: Box of 12 1-ounce bags for $4.20 or 12.5-ounce box for $2.75?

Apple juice: 128-ounce for $5.12 or 59-ounce for $3.54?

Lesson 3.4 Unit Rates in the Real World

A group of friends are training to run a race. They timed a practice session to compare their run times. Use unit rates to determine who ran the fastest.

Name	Distance	Time
Jane	$1\frac{1}{2}$ miles	$\frac{1}{3}$ hour
Rodriguez	2 miles	$\frac{2}{5}$ hour
Shanna	3.2 miles	30 minutes
Byron	0.5 miles	$\frac{1}{12}$ hour
Ellen	$2\frac{1}{3}$ miles	$\frac{2}{3}$ hour

_____ is the fastest runner.

How long would it take for the fastest runner to finish a 5-mile race if he or she ran at the same rate that he or she practiced?

NAME _____

Lesson 3.5   Fractions, Decimals, and Percents

$\frac{25}{100}$ can also be written as twenty-five hundredths (0.25).

$\frac{4}{25}$ is equivalent to $\frac{16}{100}$. This can be written as 16 hundredths (0.16).

Percent means "per 100." $\frac{25}{100}$ is equivalent to 25%.

In 2013, the trash collected in Middleville included paper; yard waste and food; plastics; metals; rubber; leather; textiles; wood; glass; and other items.

Complete the table below that shows how much of each type of trash was collected.

	Fraction	Decimal	Percent
Paper	$\frac{27}{100}$		
Yard waste and food	$\frac{14}{50}$		
Plastics		0.13	
Metals		0.09	
Rubber, leather, and textiles			9%
Wood	$\frac{3}{50}$		
Glass	$\frac{1}{20}$		
Other			3%

Spectrum Critical Thinking for Math
Grade 6
36

Lesson 3.5
Fractions, Decimals, and Percents

Lesson 3.6 Using a Bar Model to Find Percent

There are 30 students in Mr. Freeman's room. 40% of them are wearing shorts. How many students are wearing shorts?

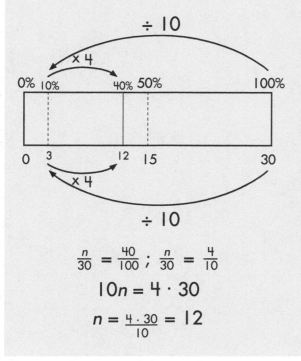

$$\frac{n}{30} = \frac{40}{100} \; ; \; \frac{n}{30} = \frac{4}{10}$$

$$10n = 4 \cdot 30$$

$$n = \frac{4 \cdot 30}{10} = 12$$

The top of the bar model goes from 0% to 100%, while the bottom goes from 0 to 30.

50% is $\frac{1}{2}$ of 100%, so 50% is 15. That is a little more than the 40% we are trying to determine.

Use relationships that are easy to find to get to 40%. 100% divided by 10 is 10% and 10% times 4 is 40%. Repeat with 30. 30 divided by 10 is 3, and 3 times 4 is 12.

12 students are wearing shorts.

220 students at Baldwin Middle School were surveyed by their teachers. Use bar models to find how many students play an instrument, and how many eat fruit at lunch. Show your work.

- 25% play an instrument.

- 70% eat fruit at lunch.

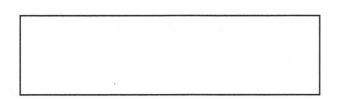

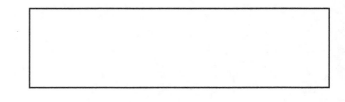

Lesson 3.6   Using a Bar Model to Find Percent

The 240 students at Creekside Middle School surveyed each other. Use bar models to find how many of the students listen to music, have more than 2 siblings, and watch TV after 8 p.m. Show your work.

- 95% listen to music.
- 12.5% have more than 2 siblings.
- 37.5% watch TV after 8 p.m.

Lesson 3.7   Percents in the Real World

Rochelle is at the store looking for the best prices. What is the best deal? Solve the problems and show your work.

Laundry detergent: $10.89 for 99 ounces, or $15.00 with 8% off for 138 ounces

Paper towels: $8.88 for 6 rolls of 74 sheets, or $18.00 for 12 rolls of 60 sheets at 20% off

Shampoo: 16.9 ounces for $10.14, or 34 ounces for $22.00 with 15% off

Check What You Learned

Ratios, Rates, and Percents

1. There are 4 counselors for every 22 students at the wilderness camp. Complete the following table with equivalent ratios:

Counselors	4		12			
Students	22	44		88		

2. What is the best buy?

	Size (oz.)	Price ($)
Snack Size Bag	2	1.88
Family Size Bag	10.25	4.92

Check What You Learned

Ratios, Rates, and Percents

3. The librarian is rearranging the books on the shelves. Now, 0.4 of the shelves are adult fiction, 38% of the shelves hold nonfiction, and $\frac{9}{20}$ of the shelves hold children's books. Which type of book uses the most shelf space?

4. Shanice is saving to buy a new jacket that costs $52. She has saved 45% of the money that she needs. How much more money does she need to save?

5. Greta bought a television on sale for 20% off the original price. The original price was $60 more than the sale price. What was the original price of the television?

NAME _____

Check What You Know

Integer Concepts

1. It was −4° F on one winter morning. The weather forecast said that it would be −8° F the next morning. Paul told his brother that it was going to be warmer the next morning. Was he right? Use the number line to show your answer.

2. Describe how to find 3 on a number line. Explain how to find the opposite of 3 on a number line. Put your results on the number line below.

3. Find the absolute value:

$|-31| =$ _____ $|100| =$ _____ $|-4.7| =$ _____

Check What You Know

Integer Concepts

4. Write an integer to represent each real-world scenario.

   a) A withdrawal of $200 _____   c) A $50 credit _____

   b) 3 mph over the speed limit _____   d) 50 feet below sea level _____

5. The social studies class is making a map of the park. Graph and label the following coordinates on the coordinate plane:

   Swing Set (–4, 3) A   Slides (–3, –1) C   Benches (–1, 1) & (–1, –1) e f
   Picnic Tables (3,2) B   Pond (5, –4) D   Parking Lot (5, 4) G

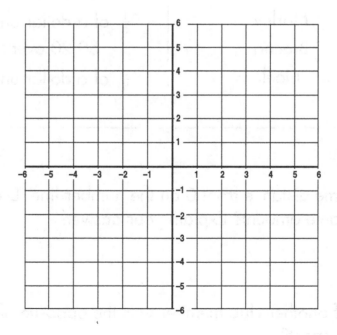

Lesson 4.1 Number Lines and Opposites

Negative numbers are found to the left of zero on a horizontal number line.
Positive numbers are found to the right of zero.

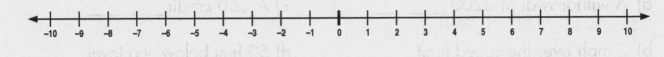

Opposite numbers are the same distance from 0, but in opposite directions.

Each Craft Club member had a budget of $5 to create a craft for the Craft
Challenge. They want to create a number line to see how each student did with the
budget. The 0 on the number line represents spending exactly $5.

Use the information below to complete the number line:

Club Member Name	Budget Status
Jade	$0.10 over
Marley	$\frac{1}{5}$ of a dollar under
Brenna	$0.20 over
Noel	$\frac{3}{4}$ of a dollar under

Two points are the same distance from 0 on the number line. Did these two club
members spend the same amount? Explain your answer.

If the budget status of another club member was the opposite of Noel's, how much
would he or she have spent?

Lesson 4.2   Number Lines and Absolute Value

Absolute value is the distance between a number and zero on a number line.

Numbers that are opposites will have the same absolute value.

$|2| = 2$

$|-2| = 2$

A group of friends is playing hide-and-seek. Their position in relation to home base is plotted on the number line.

Which two friends are the same distance from home base?

What is the absolute value of each of their positions?

Who is twice as far as Ty from the home base?

Plot a new point on the number line that has the same absolute value as the person who is twice as far as Ty.

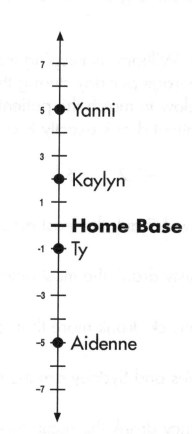

Lesson 4.3   Comparing and Ordering Integers

A group of students had a goal to eat 10 cups of fruits and vegetables daily. These numbers represent how far they were away from their goal:

$$-4.8, \frac{3}{2}, -5, 3.2$$

Put the numbers in order from least to greatest.

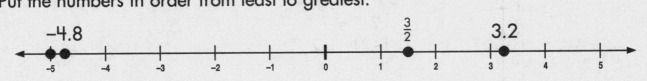

Least to greatest: $-5, -4.8, \frac{3}{2}, 3.2$

Dr. Williams is keeping track of how many cups of water her patients are drinking on average per day during the week. The goal is 8 cups of water. Use the information below to match the patient's name with the amount he or she drank. Zero means a patient drank exactly 8 cups of water a day.

$$-7.2 \qquad 6\frac{1}{2} \qquad -3 \qquad -4.5 \qquad 2 \qquad 0 \qquad 10\frac{3}{4} \qquad -6\frac{1}{2}$$

Jewel drank the least amount of water. _____

Misty drank the most amount of water. _____

Derrick drank more than Stacy, but less than Sydney. _____

Wes and Sydney are the same distance from the 8-cup goal. _____

Stacy drank the recommended amount of water each day. _____

Kadrian didn't drink as much as Ayana. _____

Lesson 4.4   Integers in the Coordinate Plane

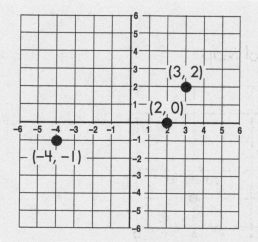

When plotting points on the coordinate grid, always start at the origin (0, 0).

The *x*-coordinate tells how many units to travel to the left (negative) or right (positive).

The *y*-coordinate tells how many units to travel up (positive) or down (negative).

Plot the following points on a coordinate grid.

(–1, 0)   (–3, 2)   (1, 3)   (0, –1)   (–2, 4)

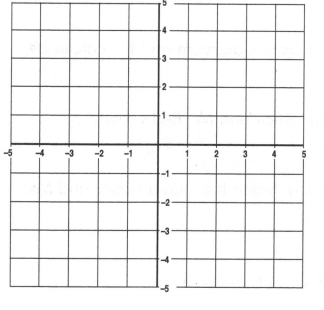

Which point is farthest left?

_____

Which point lies on the *x*-axis?

_____

Which point lies on the *y*-axis?

_____

Which point is the farthest right?

_____

Which point is closest to the top of the graph?

_____

Lesson 4.5   Coordinates in the Real World

Answer the questions using the coordinate plane.

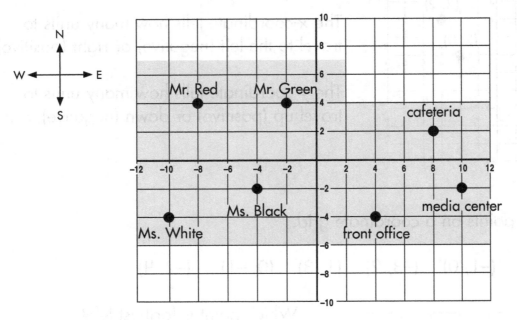

Baldwin Middle School Map

What is the horizontal distance between Ms. Black's classroom and the cafeteria?

What is the vertical distance between the front office and Mr. Red's room?

What are the vertical and horizontal distances between the media center and Ms. White's room?

Which two points have the largest vertical distance between them?

NAME _____

Check What You Learned

Integer Concepts

1. Jacob said his account balance was −$20. Ed said his account balance was −$15. Jacob thinks his account is worth more than Ed's account. Ed thinks his account is worth more than Jacob's. Who is right? Use a number line to show your answer.

2. If zero lies between w and z, give a possible set of values for w, x, y, and z.

3. The melting point of hydrogen is −259°C. The melting point of sodium is about 98°C. Which temperature has the lowest absolute value?

4. At the start of the day, there were 30 students in the classroom. That number grew and shrank throughout the day. The integers 4, −1, −2, and 0 represent the change in the number of students in the classroom. List the integers in order from least to greatest. Explain the meaning of zero in this situation.

Spectrum Critical Thinking for Math
Grade 6

Chapter 4
Check What You Learned

CHAPTER 4 POSTTEST

Check What You Learned

Integer Concepts

5. Write an integer to represent each real-world scenario, then order the integers from least to greatest.

   a) A deposit of $52 _____

   b) Club gains 1 member _____

   c) A $100 debt _____

   d) 1,000 feet above sea level _____

6. Using the grid of the town below, show how you could travel from the school to the gym along the grid lines. Each unit represents $\frac{1}{2}$ mile. Use units and direction in your answer. You may only change direction once.

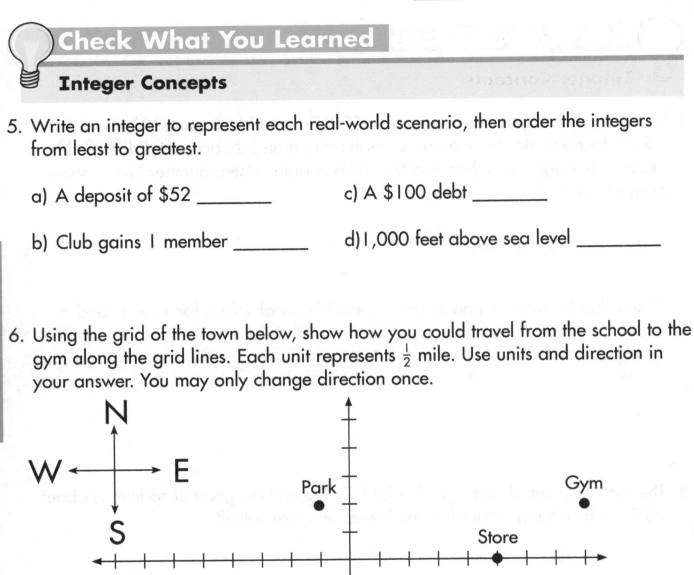

Mid-Test Chapters 1–4

1. During their last vacation, the McCoy family spent $515.72 in 4 days on food. They want to spend the same amount per day on food for this year's vacation. This year, they will take a 6-day vacation. What will be their total food cost?

2. A group of sixth grade students from Parkview Middle School went to the science museum. They were divided into 15 equal groups. There were 11 total students in each group. There were 6 boys in each group. Use the distributive property to write a number sentence to show how many boys, girls, and total students were on the trip.

_____ · (_____ + _____) =

3. At music camp, 14 counselors and 42 students will be split into groups. Each group must have the same number of students and counselors. What is the largest number of groups that can be made?

Mid-Test Chapters 1–4

4. Tara has collected 45 state quarters. If $\frac{2}{5}$ of her collection are dated 2007, what is the approximate value of the quarters from 2007?

5. A picture is $4\frac{2}{3}$ inches wide. It is being enlarged to $3\frac{1}{2}$ times its original size. What is the width of the enlarged picture?

6. Jackie is hanging glow-in-the-dark wallpaper in the game room. He needs $24\frac{2}{3}$ feet of wallpaper to cover all of the space that he wants to glow in the dark. The wallpaper comes in rolls that are $1\frac{3}{4}$ feet wide. How many rolls of wallpaper will he need to put up?

7. The ratio of black to white marbles in a bag is 3:4. If you take out 3 black marbles and 6 white ones, the ratio is 6:7. How many white marbles were originally in the bag?

8. A bus was traveling 70 feet per second. How many miles will the bus travel in 2.4 hours if it drives the same speed the entire time? Round to the nearest tenth. There are 5,280 feet in one mile.

9. Graph each fraction, percent, or decimal on the number line.

$\frac{3}{5}$ 25% $\frac{60}{200}$ 0.15   90%

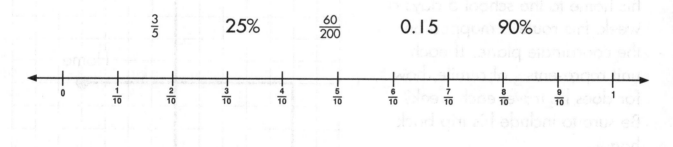

10. Sherry bought a shirt that was on sale for 20% off. She had a student discount card, so she got an additional 10% off the sale price. If the original price of the shirt was $25, how much did she pay for the shirt?

Mid-Test Chapters 1–4

11. The table shows points earned for each action in a video game. Assume that Justice started with zero points. Use a number line to determine his final score if he found a hidden treasure, reached a dead end, found a secret passage, climbed a magic staircase, and then got caught in a trap.

Action	Points
Climb a magic staircase	+3
Find a secret passage	+6
Find a hidden treasure	+9
Reach a dead end	−3
Get caught in a trap	−9

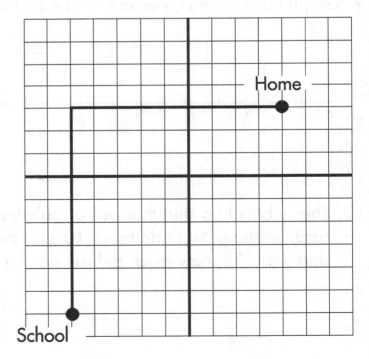

12. Mr. Washington travels from his home to the school 5 days a week. His route is mapped on the coordinate plane. If each unit represents $\frac{1}{3}$ of a mile, how far does he travel each week? Be sure to include his trip back home.

Check What You Know

Expressions and Equations

1. Rewrite as a product: $4^4 =$ _____

    $(\frac{1}{2})^3 =$ _____

2. Rewrite using exponents: $11 \cdot 11 \cdot 11 \cdot 11 \cdot 11 =$ _____

    $7 \cdot 7 \cdot 7 =$ _____

3. Write using scientific notation: $80,000 =$ _____

4. Evaluate the expression: $2 \cdot 4^2 + 3(5 + 1) \div 6 =$ _____

5. Write each phrase as an algebraic expression:

    a. 10 less than x

    _____

    b. k represents Kayla's test grade. She made 10 points higher on her 2nd test.

    _____

    c. The product of 7 and m

    _____

6. Write an equivalent expression for each:

    $3(x + 7)$ _____ $4x + x + 2x$ _____

7. What is the **6** in the expression $6x$? _____

Check What You Know

Expressions and Equations

8. Solve for x: $x + 5 = 27$

9. Solve for x: $y - 7 > 27$

10. Solve for x: $7x = 35$

11. Solve for x: $\frac{x}{3} \leq 15$

13. Tamar is two years older than Zane.

t = Tamar's age z = Zane's age

_____ is the independent variable.

_____ is the dependent variable.

Write an equation to describe the relationship.

Lesson 5.1 Order of Operations

The **order of operations** is a set of rules used to simplify numeric expressions that have more than one operation.

$(10 + 15) \div 5 + 2^2$

1. Perform operations within **parentheses**.	$(25) \div 5 + 2^2$ **(10 + 15 = 25)**
2. Find values of numbers with **exponents**.	$25 \div 5 + 4$ **(2^2 = 4)**
3. **Multiply** and **divide** from left to right.	$5 + 4$ **(25 ÷ 5 = 5)**
4. **Add** and **subtract** from left to right.	9 **(5 + 4 = 9)**

Solve the problems using the order of operations. Show your work.

$7^2 - (4 + 2 \cdot 2) \cdot 6$

$96 - 6 + 16 \div 4^2$

$(35 \div 5) \cdot 4 - 6 + 2^3$

Lesson 5.2 Scientific Notation

Scientific notation is a shortcut way to write very large numbers using the powers of 10.

10^2	$10 \cdot 10$	100
10^3	$10 \cdot 10 \cdot 10$	1,000
10^4	$10 \cdot 10 \cdot 10 \cdot 10$	10,000
10^5	$10 \cdot 10 \cdot 10 \cdot 10 \cdot 10$	100,000
10^6	$10 \cdot 10 \cdot 10 \cdot 10 \cdot 10 \cdot 10$	1,000,000

$40,000 = 4 \cdot 10,000 = 4 \times 10^4$

Write the following values using scientific notation.

1. The speed of sound is approximately 800 miles per hour.

2. The state of Colorado covers approximately 100,000 square miles.

3. The cost to attend Princeton University is approximately $60,000 per year.

4. The distance from New York to Los Angeles is over 2,000 miles.

Lesson 5.3   Algebraic Expressions

An **algebraic expressions** is made up of variables, numbers, and operations such as addition or multiplication.

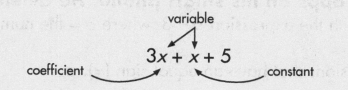

variable

$$3x + x + 5$$

coefficient · · · · · · · · · · · · · · · · · · · constant

Write the number 21 as a sum of two terms.

Write an algebraic expression containing a variable and a constant that represents the number of pencils you would have if you bought two more pencils. Let a represent the number of pencils that you have.

Let c represent pieces of candy. Each piece of candy costs $0.50. Write an expression using a coefficient and variable that represents the cost of an unknown quantity of candy.

Lesson 5.4 Expressions and Equations in the Real World

Expressions are made up of terms.

Mario had some apps on his smart phone. He deleted 3 apps.
This can be shown with the expression $a - 3$, where a = the number of apps.

Equations are expressions that have an equal sign (=).

Louis had 3 times as many apps as Mario until he downloaded 4 more apps.
This can be shown with the equation $l = 3m + 4$, where l = the number of apps that Louis has, and m = the number of apps that Mario has.

Write an expression or equation to represent each real-world scenario.

A teacher brings bookmarks for her students. She wants to give an equal number to each student. How many will she give to each student?

Rita needs 6 more shirts than the ones she already has. How many shirts does she need in all?

Joe builds cornhole games. He takes 4 hours to make each game. Joe worked on creating games for 36 hours last week. How many cornhole games did he build?

Lesson 5.5   Writing Equivalent Expressions

The commutative and associative properties allow us to rewrite algebraic expressions in order to solve problems.

Amani has two sisters, Starr and Brianna. Starr is 1 year older than Amani. Brianna is 4 years older than Amani. What is the sum of the three sisters' ages?

The age of each person can be represented by an algebraic expression:

Amani: x Star: $x + 1$ Brianna: $x + 4$

The sum of each person's age can be represented by the algebraic expression:

$$x + (x + 1) + (x + 4)$$

We can use the commutative and associative properties of addition to change the order and the grouping to rewrite the expression:

$$(x + x + x) + (1 + 4)$$

We can combine like terms to write the expression in simplest form:

$$3x + 5$$

The sum of their ages is $3x + 5$.

Use the commutative and associative properties to simplify the following expression: $(8x + 9) + (7x + 4)$

How would the simplified expression change if you added $2x + 1$ to the expression in the first problem?

Lesson 5.5 Writing Equivalent Expressions

Solve the problems. Show your work.

Todd and his friends are buying school supplies. They needed folders to organize their school work. Folders can be purchased individually or in packs. Todd bought 1 pack of folders and 2 individual folders. Max bought 2 packs of folders and 1 individual folder. Zane bought 4 packs of folders and 3 individual folders. Write an expression in simplest form to represent the total number of folders bought. How many folders are in a pack if Todd and his friends bought a total of 41 folders?

Ms. Arberg is shopping for uniforms for the 11 players on her volleyball team. Adams' Print Shop has jerseys for j dollars and will add a number and a logo for $3. The shorts they offer cost s dollars plus $2 for the logo. Write an expression that tells how much the uniforms will cost.

If the jerseys cost $12 without the number and logo and the shorts cost $7 without the logo, what is the total cost?

Lesson 5.6   Addition and Subtraction Equations

You can solve addition and subtraction equations using tape diagrams. Tape diagrams use rectangles to show different parts of an equation.

What number added to 3 is 11?	10 subtracted from what number is 4?
$x + 3 = 11$	$x - 10 = 4$

x	3
11	

10	4
x	

$$11 - 3 = x$$
$$x = 8$$

$$x = 10 + 4$$
$$x = 14$$

Write an equation for each description. Solve the equation using a tape diagram.

What number added to 7 is 21?

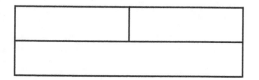

14 subtracted from what number is 7?

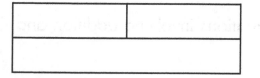

13 added to what number is 27?

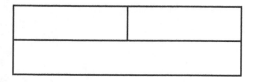

Lesson 5.6　Addition and Subtraction Equations

Write an equation for the description. Solve the equation using a tape diagram.
Show your work.

14 fewer than a number is 13.

Answer the questions.

What is the relationship between the operation in your equation and the operation you used when solving with the tape diagram?

What conclusions can you draw about how to solve equations involving addition and subtraction?

Lesson 5.7 Solving Multiplication and Division Equations

You can also solve multiplication and division equations using tape diagrams.

4 times what number is 20?

$4x = 20$

x	x	x	x
20			

$x = \frac{20}{4}$

$x = 5$

What number divided by 3 is 5?

$\frac{x}{3} = 5$

x		
5	5	5

$x = 3 \cdot 5$

$x = 15$

5 times what number is 30?

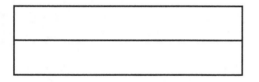

What number divided by 6 is 5?

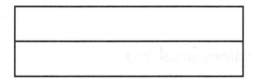

7 groups of what number is 35?

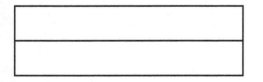

Lesson 5.7   Solving Multiplication and Division Equations

Write an equation for the description. Solve the equation using a tape diagram.
Show your work.

What number split into 5 groups is 7?

Answer the questions.

What is the relationship between the operation in your equation and the operation
you used when solving with the tape diagram?

What conclusions can you draw about how to solve equations involving
multiplication and division?

Lesson 5.8   Identifying Equivalent Equations

Equations can be solved by applying the opposite operation to each side of the equation.

$$3 + x = 7$$
$$\underline{-3 \quad\quad -3}$$
$$x = 4$$

$$\frac{m}{7} = 3$$
$$7 \cdot \frac{m}{7} = 3 \cdot 7$$
$$m = 21$$

Solve the following equations. The equations that have the same solution are equivalent. Write the equivalent equations in the table below.

$$3x = 75 \qquad\qquad x + 18 = 35 \qquad\qquad 3x = 51$$

$$9x = 81 \qquad\qquad 4 + x = 29 \qquad\qquad x - 9 = 0$$

$$x - 15 = 2 \qquad\qquad 8 + x = 17 \qquad\qquad \frac{x}{5} = 5$$

List the groups of equivalent equations.

x = _____	x = _____	x = _____

Lesson 5.9 Solving Inequalities in the Real World

Gloria needs at least $50 to buy the shoes that she wants. She has $37. How much more money does she need?

Use a **greater than or equal to sign** instead of an equal sign because Gloria needs **at least** $50.

$$x + 37 \geq 50$$
$$\underline{-37 \quad -37}$$
$$x \geq 13$$

Gloria needs at least $13.

Write and solve an inequality for each scenario. Give the reasoning for the inequality used.

Millie can have no more than 15 gallons of gas in her car. She already has 9 gallons of gas when she stops at the gas station. How much gas can she get?

Timothy walked 800 fewer steps than he walked the previous day. His fitness tracker battery died before he got home. He knows that he had walked 5,380 steps before the tracker turned off. He continued to take more steps after he got home from school. About how many steps did he walk the previous day?

Lesson 5.9 Solving Inequalities in the Real World

Write and solve an inequality for each scenario. Give the reasoning for the inequality used.

Erica has some colored pencils. She wants to divide all of the pencils equally among her 8 friends. She wants to give them fewer than 6 pencils each. How many pencils does she have?

Ray has 11 boxes of rocks in his rock collection. He knows that he has at least 132 rocks. How many rocks could be in each box if each box contains the same number of rocks?

Lamar can eat 2,000 calories a day at most. He has eaten 980 calories so far. How many more calories can he eat today?

Lesson 5.10 Variables in the Real World

Julie babysits for her neighbor. She charges $10 for each hour that she babysits. If she babysits for 3 hours, how much will she earn?

The amount that Julie is paid **depends** on the number of hours that she babysits. The variable that represents her pay is the **dependent** variable. The variable that represents the number of hours she worked is the **independent** variable.

E = babysitting earnings h = hours worked

$E = 10h$ $E = 10(3)$ $E = 30$

Julie earned $30.

Write an equation or inequality for each scenario. Identify the dependent and independent variables. Solve the equation or inequality.

Wendy is saving money in her new savings account. She saves $20 a month. After how many months will she have $180 saved?

Tiffany has a goal to read at least 150 pages in a week. It's the last day of the week and she has read 138 pages. How many more pages does Tiffany need to read to meet or exceed her goal?

Lesson 5.10 Variables in the Real World

Write an equation or inequality for each scenario. Identify the dependent and independent variables. Solve the equation or inequality.

Gerald buys gum for himself and his two friends. How many pieces of gum did he buy if he and each of his friends get 7 pieces?

Oranges are on sale at the fruit stand. Juanita bought a bag of oranges for $5.35. The sale price was $1.50 less than the regular price. What was the regular price?

Callie earns $8.50 an hour doing odd jobs for neighbors. Her neighbor can pay her at most $51 to do some work at her house. How many hours can Callie work?

Check What You Learned

Expressions and Equations

1. Harrison's baseball team uses a phone tree when a game is cancelled. The team mom calls 2 players. Each of those players calls 2 players, and so on. How many players will be called during the 4th round of calls?

2. Evaluate the expression: $3(10 + 3) \div (8 + 5) + 6 \cdot 4^2$

3. Write each phrase as an algebraic expression:

   a. m less than 4

   _____

   b. b represents Briana's savings total before a deposit. She deposits $30 into her account.

   _____

   c. The quotient of 7 and m

   _____

   d. h represents the number of hours that Eugene works. What is his pay if he makes $8.50 per hour?

   _____

4. Write an equivalent expression for:

   $11(x + 4) =$ _____

   $10x - x + 4x =$ _____

5. What is the **10** in the expression $10 + x$? _____

Check What You Learned

Expressions and Equations

6. Solve for j: $6 + j = 27$.

7. Solve for x: $5x = 80$.

8. Solve for y: $y - 7 > 27$

9. Solve for x: $\frac{x}{3} \leq 15$

10. Mariah is $2\frac{3}{4}$ times as old as Rhianna.

    m = Mariah's age; r = Rhianna's age

    _____ is the independent variable.   _____ is the dependent variable.

    Write an equation to describe the relationship: _____

NAME _____

Check What You Know

Geometry

Find the area of each figure.

1.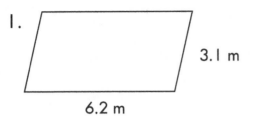

3.1 m

6.2 m

2.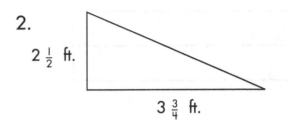

$2\frac{1}{2}$ ft.

$3\frac{3}{4}$ ft.

3.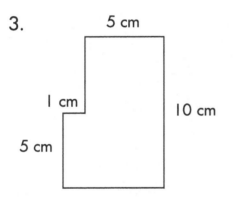

5 cm

1 cm

5 cm

10 cm

4.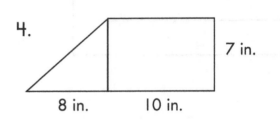

7 in.

8 in.   10 in.

Find the volume of each figure.

5.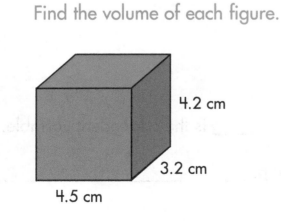

4.2 cm

3.2 cm

4.5 cm

6.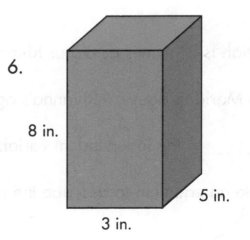

8 in.

5 in.

3 in.

Check What You Know

Geometry

7. Find the surface area of each figure.

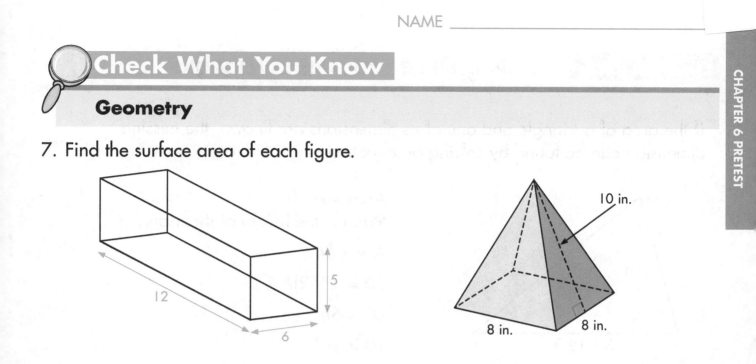

8. A square is formed by the points A (−3, 2), B (2, 2), C (−3, −3), and an unknown point D. Where does D fall?

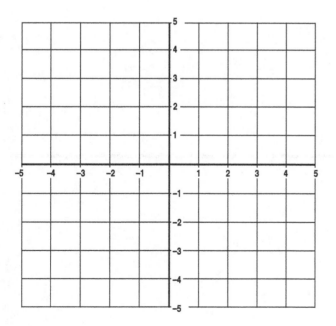

Lesson 6.1 Finding Dimensions of a Triangle

If the area of a triangle and one of its dimensions are known, the missing dimension can be found by solving an equation.

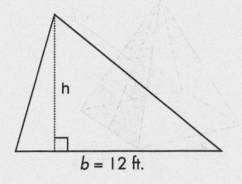

Area = 60 ft.^{2}
What is the height of the triangle?

$A = \frac{1}{2}bh$

$60 = \frac{1}{2}(12)h$

$60 = 6h$

$10 \text{ ft.} = h$

$b = 12$ ft.

Find the missing dimension.

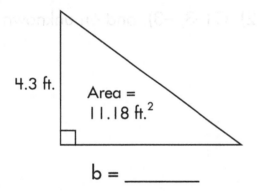

4.3 ft.

Area = 11.18 ft.^{2}

b = _____

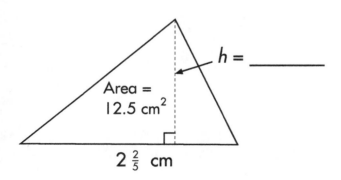

Area = 12.5 cm^2

$h =$ _____

$2\frac{2}{5}$ cm

Lesson 6.2   Finding the Area of Quadrilaterals

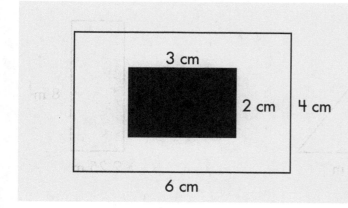

What is the area of the mirror's frame?

Total area = 4 cm x 6 cm = 24 cm^2
Mirror area = 3 cm x 2 cm = 6 cm^2

Area of the frame = 24 cm^2 − 6 cm^2
= 18 cm^2

Use the figures to answer the questions.

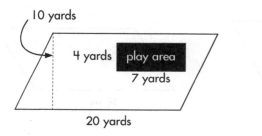

What is the area of the grassy part of the yard outside the play area?

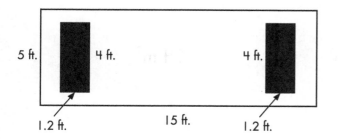

What is the area of the wall, not including the two windows?

Lesson 6.3   Finding the Area of Other Polygons

Find the area of each polygon.

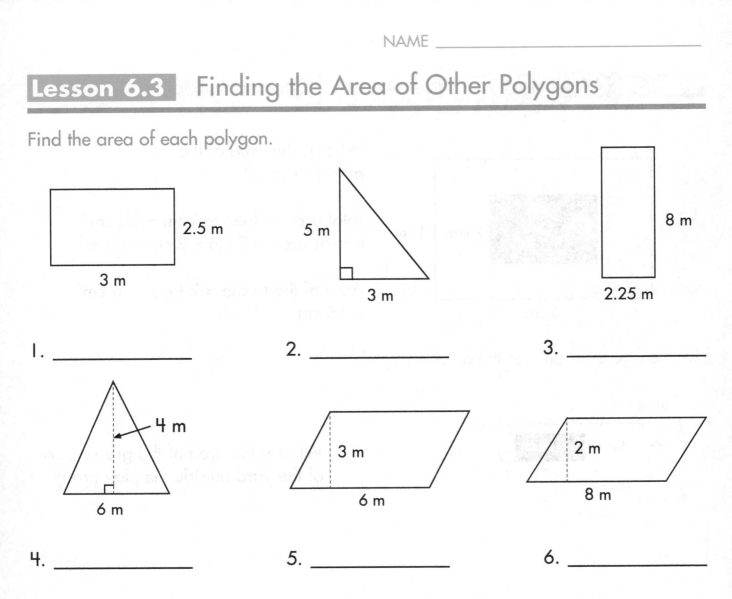

1. _____

2. _____

3. _____

4. _____

5. _____

6. _____

Now, combine the polygons above into figures with each area given below, using each polygon only once. Draw the composite shape formed by combining the polygons.

30 m^2 15 m^2 34 m^2

Lesson 6.4 Volume of Rectangular Solids

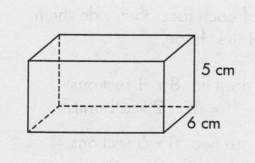

The volume of a rectangular prism is 210 cm^3. If it has a height of 5 cm and a width of 6 cm, what is the length?

$V = 210$ cm^3
$210 = (5)(6) \, l; \; 210 = 30 \, l$
$l = 7$ cm

Find the missing dimensions.

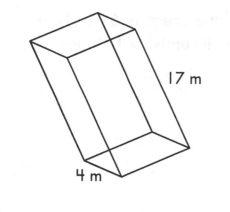

17 m

4 m

$V = 680$ m^3

2 m

2.5 m

$V = 15.625$ m^3

What is the length of a cereal box that can hold 228 in.^{3} and has a width of $2\frac{1}{2}$ inches and a height of $7\frac{5}{8}$ inches?

Lesson 6.5   Using a Net to Find Surface Area

A **net** is a flattened-out 3-D shape. Find the area of each face, then add them together. The sum of the faces is the surface area of the shape.

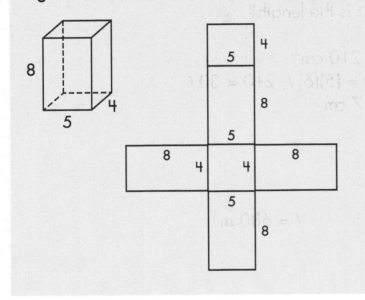

There are two, 8 x 4 sections:
$A = 8 \cdot 4 = 32 \cdot 2 = 64$ units^2

There are two, 8 x 5 sections:
$A = 8 \cdot 5 = 40 \cdot 2 = 80$ units^2

There are two , 4 x 5 sections:
$A = 20 \cdot 2 = 40$ units^2

The sum of the areas is 64 units^2 + 80 units^2 + 40 units^2 = 184 units^2

Draw a net for each 3-D object. Use the net to calculate the surface area.

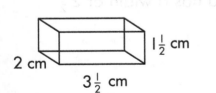

6 in.

4 in.   2 in.

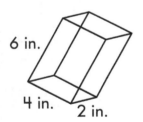

2 cm

$3\frac{1}{2}$ cm

$1\frac{1}{2}$ cm

Lesson 6.5   Using a Net to Find Surface Area

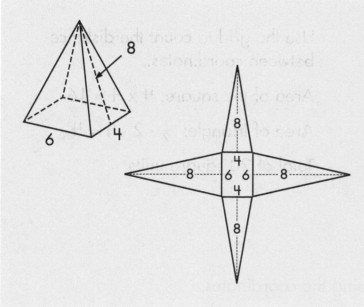

The base is 6 x 4:
A = 6 · 4 = 24 units²

Two triangles have a base of 6 units and a height of 8 units:
A = ½ · 6 · 8   24 · 2 = 48 units²

Two triangles have a base of 4 units and a height of 8 units:
A = ½ · 4 · 8   16 · 2 = 32 units²

The sum of the areas is 24 units² + 48 units² + 32 units² = 104 units²

Draw a net for the 3-D object. Use the net to calculate the surface area.

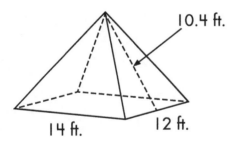

10.4 ft.

14 ft.   12 ft.

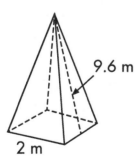

9.6 m

2 m

Lesson 6.6 Area on the Coordinate Plane

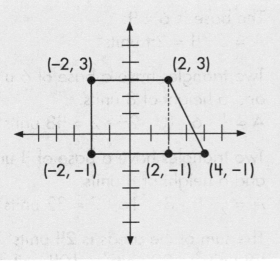

Use the grid to count the distance between coordinates.

Area of the square: 4 x 4 = 16

Area of triangle: $\frac{1}{2} \cdot 2 \cdot 4 = 4$

Total of 20 square units

Find the area of the composite shapes using the coordinates.

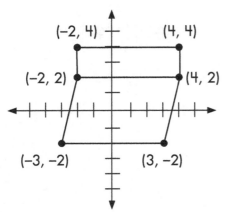

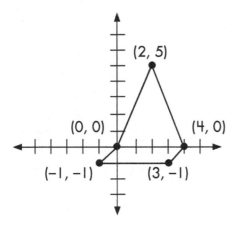

Check What You Learned

Geometry

1. Find the missing dimension.

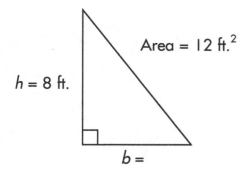

Area = 12 ft.^{2}

$h = 8$ ft.

$b =$

2. Find the area.

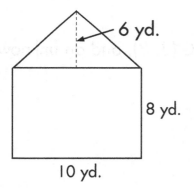

6 yd.

8 yd.

10 yd.

3. Find the missing dimension.

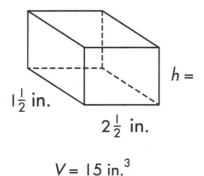

$h =$

$1\frac{1}{2}$ in.

$2\frac{1}{2}$ in.

$V = 15$ in.^{3}

Check What You Learned

Geometry

4. Find the surface area.

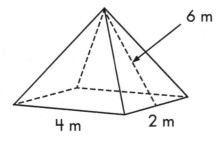

5. A square is formed by the points A (3, –2), B (–2, –2), C (3, 3), and an unknown point D. Where does D fall?

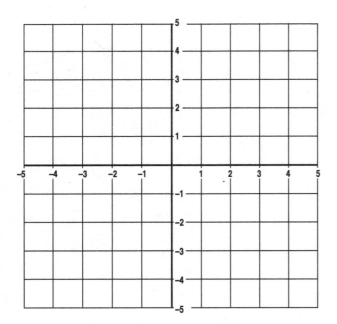

Check What You Know

Probability and Statistics

1. The ages of the 6 people taking a water aerobics class are 34, 66, 22, 55, 23, and 77.

   a. Find the mean. Round to the nearest hundredth.

   b. Find the median.

   c. Find the mode.

   d. Find the range.

   e. Find the mean absolute deviation (MAD). Round your answer to the nearest tenth.

Check What You Know

Probability and Statistics

2. Create data displays for the data set at the top of the previous page.

   a. Create a stem and leaf plot.

   b. Create a histogram.

   c. Create a box and whisker plot.

Lesson 7.1 Mean, Median, and Mode

Measures of center (mean, median, mode) are used to describe and analyze a data set. Measures of center summarize all of a data set's values with a single number.

Scientists collected height data from a group of 6th graders. Find the mean and median height of the group.

6th Grade Students' Heights (inches): 79, 54, 51, 59, 63, 55, 59

The **mean** is the average value of the set. To find it, add all of the values and divide the sum by the number of values. A value that is much lower or higher is an **outlier**. Outliers can distort the mean and show a misleading picture of the data. In this set, 79 is an outlier.

Mean Height: $\dfrac{(79+54+51+59+63+55+59)}{7} = 60$

The mean is 60 inches.

The **median** is a data set's middle number. To find it, order the values from least to greatest and find the middle number. For an even number of values, the median is the mean of the 2 middle numbers. If a set has an outlier, the median may be a more accurate measure of center than the mean.

Median Height: 51 54 55 (59) 59 63 79. The median is 59 inches.

The **mode** is the value that appears most frequently in the data set. Here, the mode is 59.

Lesson 7.1 Mean, Median, and Mode

Find the mean and median of each data set.

# of Letters in First Name				
3	8	8	4	10
3	3	9	3	7

# of Letters in Last Name				
5	7	5	6	5
5	11	20	9	9

Is the mean or the median a better measure of center for last names? Explain your answer.

Lesson 7.2   Measures of Variability: Range and MAD

Measures of variability (including **range** and **mean absolute deviation**) describe how the values in a data set vary.

Calculate the range and mean absolute deviation of the height data.

6th Grade Students' Heights (inches): 79, 54, 51, 59, 63, 55, 59

79, 54, **51**, 59, 63, 55, 59
Range: 79 – 51 = 28 inches

- Range is the difference between the largest and smallest values in the data set.

$|51 - 60| = 9$ $|54 - 60| = 6$ $|55 - 60| = 5$

$|59 - 60| = 1$ $|59 - 60| = 1$ $|63 - 60| = 3$

$|79 - 60| = 19$

- To calculate mean absolute deviation, find the absolute value of the difference between the mean of the data set and each value in the set. Then, find the mean of the absolute values.

$$MAD = \frac{(9 + 1 + 19 + 6 + 1 + 5 + 3)}{7} = 6.3$$

The closer the mean absolute deviation of a data set is to zero, the more consistent the set is.

The players on the basketball team are 65, 72, 67, 71, 73, 63, and 69 inches tall. Find the range and mean absolute deviation of the data set. Round your answers to the nearest hundredth.

If a new player who is 85 inches tall joins the team, how will his height affect the range and mean absolute deviation of the data set?

Lesson 7.3   Analyzing Data in the Real World

Answer the questions. Show your work.

Jesse and Malik mow lawns to earn money for soccer uniforms. Last week, they mowed 7 lawns and made $168. The range of the amounts they were paid was $32. For 6 of the lawns, they were paid $19, $33, $27, $25, $34, and $28.

How much were Jesse and Malik paid for the 7th lawn?

Find the mean and median of the data. Which measure gives you the most accurate picture of how the data is distributed?

Find the mean absolute deviation of the data set. Which value is the outlier?

The person who paid Jesse and Malik the least gave them an extra $20. What is the range of the new data set? How would the new number change the mean absolute deviation of the data set?

Lesson 7.4 Box Plots

Box plots display data along a number line and divide it into **quartiles**, or quarters. Each section of the plot shows 25 percent of the data.

Make a box plot to show the height data.

6th Grade Students' Heights (inches): 79, 54, 51, 59, 63, 55, 59

- Arrange the numbers in order: 51, 54, 55, 59, 59, 63, 79. The median is **59**. The minimum value is **51**, and the maximum value is **79**.

- The lower quartile, or Q1, is the median of the lower half of the data: 51, **54**, 55.

- The upper quartile, or Q3, is the median of the upper half of the data: 59, **63**, 79.

- Plot each value above a number line. Draw a box around the median with its ends going through the quartiles.

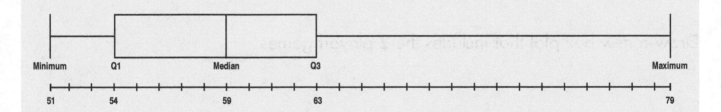

The graph shows that about half of the data in the set is distributed almost equally around the median. The outlier is clearly separated. This allows you to see the rest of the data in a way that is not distorted by the outlier.

Lesson 7.4 Box Plots

The Carroll Cougars won 9 basketball games by 3, 2, 7, 15, 2, 4, 11, 1, and 6 points. Make a box plot for the data set.

The Cougars won 2 playoff games by 9 and 12 points. If you added these games to the data set, how would the box plot change?

Draw a new box plot that includes the 2 playoff games.

Lesson 7.5   Stem and Leaf Plots

A data set can be organized into a **stem and leaf plot** by using place values. Each number in the set is converted to tens and ones. The tens digits are the stems and the ones digits are the leaves.

Make a stem and leaf plot to show the height data.
6th Grade Students' Heights (inches): 79, 54, 51, 59, 63, 55, 59

This allows you to easily see the minimum (51), the maximum (79), the range (28), and the median (59).

Stem	Leaves
5	1 4 5 9 9
6	3
7	9

Elian has scored 77, 82, 85, 75, 91, 85, 82, 89, 87, and 94 on his math tests this year. Draw a stem and leaf plot to show Elian's scores. Find the median and the range.

There is one more test on the last day of school, and it changes the mean of Elian's test scores to 86. What is Elian's final test score? What is the new range of the data?

Lesson 7.6 Histograms

Histograms show the distribution of data by grouping data within a certain range and graphing the frequency of data points in the range.

Make a histogram to show the height data.

6th Grade Students' Heights (inches): 79, 54, 51, 59, 63, 55, 59

The histogram shows that most of the height values are grouped in the 50–59 range.

Construct a histogram for the data set.

Test 1 Grades:
46, 40, 98, 72, 89, 88, 79, 67, 78, 91, 43, 53, 77, 81, 75, 76, 89

Predict which range the mean will fall in.

Explain your prediction. Then, calculate the mean to the nearest tenth. Were you correct?

NAME _____

Check What You Learned

Probability and Statistics

The box plots below compare the amount of candy per bag for two brands of chocolate candy.

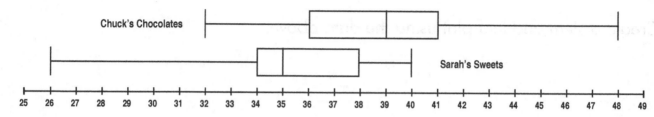

1. What conclusions can you draw about the amount of candies per bag for each brand?

2. What percentage of Chuck's Chocolates bags contain 39 or more candies?

The histogram below is based on this data set of sixth graders' weights: 56, 58, 66, 63, 64, 62, 71, 77, 84, 84, 88, 91.

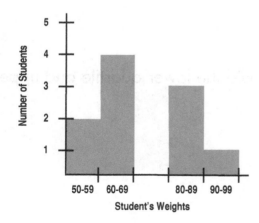

3. Fill in the missing range and draw the missing bar.

4. How many students weigh between 50 and 79 pounds?

Check What You Learned

Probability and Statistics

Ms. Hutchings posted her sixth-grade students' test grades on the class website: 57, 98, 62, 74, 77, 91, 85, 88, 81, 92, 69, 50, 83, 79, 91, 85, 78, 89, 90, 80, 68.

5. Create a stem and leaf plot using the data above.

6. Find the mean, median, and range of the data. Round to the nearest tenth.

7. If this data was shown with a box plot, what would the lower quartile and upper quartile be?

Final Test Chapters 1–7

1. Michael is shopping at the hardware store. He has $19. Does he have enough to buy 3 treated 2 x 4 lumber planks, 2.5 pounds of nails, and 1 can of wood stain?

Item	Price
Treated 2 x 4 lumber planks	$2.87
1 lb. of nails	$4.78
Can of wood stain	$7.77

2. William borrowed $1,014 from his grandparents to pay for his new laptop. He plans to give his grandparents $84 a month until he has paid back the full cost. How much will his last payment to his grandparents be?

3. Carpet is need to cover the room pictured below. The carpet costs $5.27 per square foot. How much will it cost to buy the carpet?

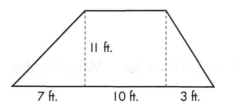

11 ft.

7 ft.   10 ft.   3 ft.

Final Test Chapters 1–7

4. Carla ran $3\frac{1}{2}$ miles for every $2\frac{3}{4}$ miles that Skip ran. Complete the ratio table below.

Carla's Distance	$3\frac{1}{2}$ miles	7 miles		
Skip's Distance	$2\frac{3}{4}$ miles		$8\frac{1}{4}$ miles	

5. McKenzie spilled 22 pints of water in 4 days. Avery collected 14 pints of water in 3 days. How many pints did each of them lose or gain per day? Show the values on the number line.

6. Explain how to find the opposite of the number that is 2 units less than −17 on the number line. Justify your answer on the number line.

7. The area of a parallelogram is 138.46 m². The height is 6.02 meters. What is the length of the base?

Final Test Chapters 1–7

8. Jeff is tracking a helicopter in his area that includes Greenville (5, 3), Burlington (1, 1), Waysville (5, 1), Pilotsboro (3, 6), Denverson (0, 4), and Henderson (3, 2). The helicopter is currently at (−3, −4) and is moving quickly toward Greenville. Which town will it fly past the soonest? Plot the points and explain your answer.

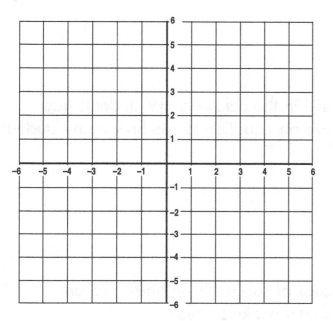

9. Use a number line to order from least to greatest: −4, −4.25, 4.125, $3\frac{3}{4}$, 2, −$\frac{1}{2}$, 4

10. 80% of sixth grade girls listen to music at least twice a day. If 320 sixth grade girls were surveyed, how many listen to music?

Final Test Chapters 1–7

11. Find the perimeter of the rectangle.

$x + 2$

$2x - 1$

12. When the bell rang, 24 students were still in the cafeteria. 49 students had already left the cafeteria. Write and solve an equation to see how many students were in the cafeteria before the end of lunch.

13. 9 dozen cookies can be made with $\frac{27}{2}$ cups of sugar. Write and solve an equation to see how many cups each dozen cookies needs.

14. Amani is taking guitar lessons. She learns 2 songs with the hopes of learning at least 5 songs for the week. Write and solve an inequality that can be used to determine how many more songs she has to learn.

CHAPTERS 1–7 FINAL TEST

Spectrum Critical Thinking for Math
Grade 6
100

Chapters 1–7
Final Test

Final Test Chapters 1–7

15. Find the area of the composite shape.

16. Find the surface area.

17. Find the volume. What are the independent and dependent variables in the volume formula?

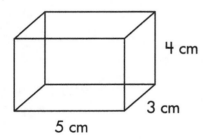

Spectrum Critical Thinking for Math
Grade 6

Chapters 1–7
Final Test
101

CHAPTERS 1–7 FINAL TEST

Final Test Chapters 1–7

Jada is practicing for a big bicycle race. She keeps track of how many miles she rides each day. Here are the distances she rode last week: 14, 17, 1, 21, 19, 16, 41.

18. What is the best way to graph this data set? Why?

19. Graph Jada's bicycle mileage using the method you chose.

20. Over the next three weeks, Jada rode these distances in miles: 18, 9, 38, 24, 33, 31, 17, 42, 44, 39, 47, 19, 26, 42, 51, 8, 50, 49, 52, 11, 51. Combine this data set with the one at the top of the page, and create a histogram to show the data.

CHAPTERS 1–7 FINAL TEST

Spectrum Critical Thinking for Math
Grade 6
102

Chapters 1–7
Final Test

Answer Key

Page 5

NAME _____

Check What You Know

Number Systems and Operations

CHAPTER 1 PRETEST

Identify the property shown.

1. $3(1+5) = 3 + 15$ ___Distributive___

2. $(4 + 7) + 6 = 4 + (7 + 6)$ ___Associative___

3. $(14 + 7) \cdot (28 + 9) = (28 + 9) \cdot (14 + 7)$ ___Commutative___

Use the distributive property to multiply.

4. $11 \cdot 39$ $39(1 + 10)$
$39 + 390$
429

5. $123 \cdot 21$ $123(20 + 1)$
$2460 + 123$
$2,583$

6. Rewrite the number sentence using subtraction: $47 + 14 = 61$

$$61 - 14 = 47 \text{ or } 61 - 47 = 14$$

7. Rewrite the number sentence using multiplication: $1417 \div 13 = 109$

$$109 \cdot 13 = 1,417$$

8. Find the least common multiple of 12 and 16.
12: 12 24 36 (48) 60
16: 16 32 (48) 64

9. Find the greatest common factor of 48 and 96.
48: 1, 2, 3, 4, 6, 8, 12, 16, 24, (48)
96: 1, 2, 3, 4, 6, 8, 12, 16, 24, 32, (48), 96

10. $16.35 \div 10.9$

$\times 10$ $\times 10$
163.5 109

$$109\overline{)163.5} \quad \begin{array}{r} 1.5 \\ -109\downarrow \\ \hline 545 \\ -545 \\ \hline 0 \end{array}$$

Page 6

NAME _____

Lesson 1.1 Applying Number Properties

Number properties allow us to rewrite algebraic expressions in order to solve problems. The **commutative properties** of **addition** and **multiplication** state that the order in which numbers are added or multiplied does not change the value of the sum or product.

$a + b = b + a$ $a \cdot b = b \cdot a$
$2 + 3 = 3 + 2$ $2 \cdot 3 = 3 \cdot 2$
$x + 7 = 7 + x$ $3 \cdot x = x \cdot 3$

The commutative property can be used to help add several numbers using mental math.

$15 + 49 + 52 + 25 + 18 + 11$ can be rewritten as:

$$15 + 25 + 49 + 11 + 52 + 18 =$$

$$40 + 60 + 70$$

$$= 170$$

Complete the equations to reflect the commutative properties.

1. $17 + 34 = \underline{34} + 17$

2. $j \cdot k = \underline{k} \cdot j$

3. $12 + 63 + 18 + 17 = 12 + \underline{18} + 17 + \underline{63}$

4. Show how mental math can be used to find this sum: $14 + 28 + 93 + 52 + 36 + 47$

$$14 + 36 + 28 + 52 + 93 + 47$$
$$50 + 80 + 140 = 270$$

Page 7

NAME _____

Lesson 1.1 Applying Number Properties

The **associative properties** of addition and multiplication state that the way the addends or factors are grouped doesn't change the value of the sum or product.

$(a + b) + c = a + (b + c)$ $(a \cdot b) \cdot c = a \cdot (b \cdot c)$
$(2 + 3) + 4 = 2 + (3 + 4)$ $(2 \cdot 3) \cdot 4 = 2 \cdot (3 \cdot 4)$
$x + (7 + 2) = (2 + x) + 7$ $(3 \cdot 4) \cdot x = (x \cdot 3) \cdot 4$

Complete the equations to reflect the associative properties.

1. $(21 \cdot 13) \cdot 24 = 21 \cdot (13 \cdot \underline{24})$

2. $(w + x) + y = \underline{w} + (x + y)$

3. $(7 \cdot 1) \cdot \underline{72} = 7 \cdot (1 \cdot 72)$

4. $(\underline{8} + 3) + 15 = 8 + (3 + \underline{15})$

5. $(10 \cdot \underline{3}) \cdot 2 = \underline{10} \cdot (3 \cdot 2)$

Page 8

NAME _____

Lesson 1.2 Distributive Property and Multiplication

The **distributive property** is the repeated addition of a sum or difference.

$a(b + c) = a \cdot b + a \cdot c$ $a(b - c) = a \cdot b - a \cdot c$
$3(2 + 5) = (3 \cdot 2) + (3 \cdot 5) = 6 + 15 = 21$ $3(6 - 2) = (3 \cdot 6) - (3 \cdot 2) =$
$18 - 6 = 12$

The distributive property can be used to find the product of multi-digit factors:
$18 \cdot 6 = \underline{}$

Rewrite 18: $10 + 8$

Multiply using the distributive property:

$6(10 + 8) = 6 \cdot 10 + 6 \cdot 8 = 60 + 48 = 108$

$$18 \cdot 6 = 108$$

Use the distributive property to find each product.

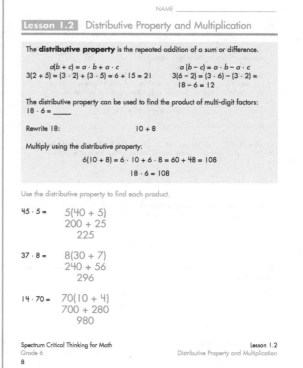

$45 \cdot 5 =$ $5(40 + 5)$
$200 + 25$
225

$37 \cdot 8 =$ $8(30 + 7)$
$240 + 56$
296

$14 \cdot 70 =$ $70(10 + 4)$
$700 + 280$
980

Page 9

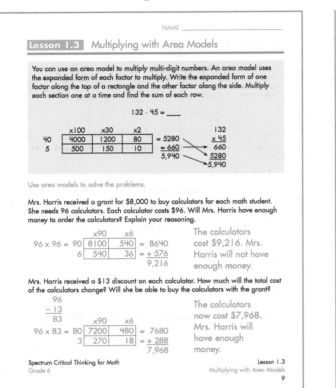

Lesson 1.3 Multiplying with Area Models

You can use an area model to multiply multi-digit numbers. An area model uses the expanded form of each factor to multiply. Write the expanded form of one factor along the top of a rectangle and the other factor along the side. Multiply each section one at a time and find the sum of each row.

132 · 45 = ____

	x100	x30	x2			132
40	4000	1200	80	= 5280		x 45
5	500	150	10	= 660		660
				5,940		5280
						5,940

Use area models to solve the problems.

Mrs. Harris received a grant for $8,000 to buy calculators for each math student. She needs 96 calculators. Each calculator costs $96. Will Mrs. Harris have enough money to order the calculators? Explain your reasoning.

	x90	x6	
96 x 96 = 90	8100	540	= 8640
6	540	36	= + 576
			9,216

The calculators cost $9,216. Mrs. Harris will not have enough money.

Mrs. Harris received a $13 discount on each calculator. How much will the total cost of the calculators change? Will she be able to buy the calculators with the grant?

```
   96
 - 13
   83
```

	x90	x6	
96 x 83 = 80	7200	480	= 7680
3	270	18	= + 288
			7,968

The calculators now cost $7,968. Mrs. Harris will have enough money.

Spectrum Critical Thinking for Math
Grade 6

Lesson 1.3
Multiplying with Area Models
9

Page 10

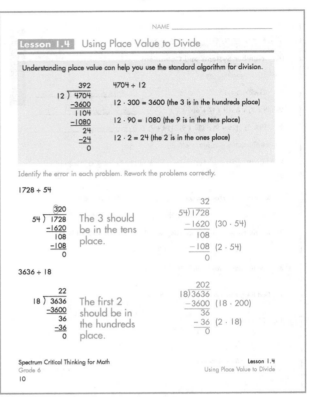

Lesson 1.4 Using Place Value to Divide

Understanding place value can help you use the standard algorithm for division.

```
        392            4704 ÷ 12
   12 ) 4704
       -3600           12 · 300 = 3600 (the 3 is in the hundreds place)
        1104
       -1080           12 · 90 = 1080 (the 9 is in the tens place)
          24
         -24           12 · 2 = 24 (the 2 is in the ones place)
           0
```

Identify the error in each problem. Rework the problems correctly.

1728 ÷ 54

```
        320
   54 ) 1728        The 3 should
       -1620        be in the tens
        108         place.
       -108
          0
```

```
         32
   54 ) 1728
       -1620   (30 · 54)
         108
        -108   (2 · 54)
           0
```

3636 ÷ 18

```
         22
   18 ) 3636        The first 2
       -3600        should be in
         36         the hundreds
        -36         place.
          0
```

```
        202
   18 ) 3636
       -3600   (18 · 200)
          36
         -36   (2 · 18)
           0
```

Spectrum Critical Thinking for Math
Grade 6
10

Lesson 1.4
Using Place Value to Divide

Page 11

Lesson 1.5 Reciprocal Operations

Multiplication and division are reciprocal, or opposite, operations. An opposite operation will "undo" the original operation.

Niki bought 8 pairs of jeans to wear to school. If her mother spent a total of $168, how much did she spend for each pair of jeans? Write two different number sentences that can be used to find the cost of one pair of jeans.

168 ÷ 8 = ? ; 8 · ? = 168

Write two different number sentences that could be used to solve each problem.

Jonathan filled 24 bags with marbles for his younger brother's class. He put 14 marbles in each bag. How many marbles did he give to his brother's class?

24 · 14 = ?
? ÷ 24 = 14

Kimberly earned 106,788 points while playing 11 rounds of a video game. What is the average number of points that she earned each game?

106788 ÷ 11 = ?
? · 11 = 106788

Ephraim can text 32 words per minute. How many words could he type if he typed for an entire hour?

32 · 60 = ?
? ÷ 60 = 32

Spectrum Critical Thinking for Math
Grade 6

Lesson 1.5
Reciprocal Operations
11

Page 12

Lesson 1.6 Greatest Common Factor

The largest number that is the factor of any set of at least 2 numbers is the **greatest common factor (GCF)**.

To find the greatest common factor of 6, 15, and 21, list the factors of each number.

6: 1, 2, 3, 6   15: 1, 3, 5, 15   21: 1, 3, 7, 21

The greatest common factor is 3.

What is a possible combination of 3 numbers with a GCF of 7?
List multiples of 7: 7, 14, 21, 28, 35, 42, 49, 56, 63, 70, 77, 84, 91, 98, 105

Choose 3 of the listed multiples.

14, 28, 42 is _not_ a possible combination. Although they all have a common factor of 7, the greatest common factor is 14.

14, 28, 35 is a possible combination. Although 14 is a common factor for 14 and 28, it is not a factor of 35; therefore 7 is the greatest common factor.

Give 2 sets of numbers that have 6 as the GCF. Explain your answer.

Answers can vary. Some examples:
6, 12
12, 18, 24   30, 36
30, 48, 60   36, 42, 48

Multiples of 6:
6, 12, 18, 24, 30,
36, 42, 48, 54, 60

Give 2 sets of numbers that have 11 as the GCF. Explain your answer.

Answers can vary. Some examples:
22, 33, 77
22, 99, 110
55, 88, 110
11, 44, 110

Multiples of 11:
11, 22, 33, 44,
55, 66, 77, 88,
99, 110

Spectrum Critical Thinking for Math
Grade 6
12

Lesson 1.6
Greatest Common Factor

Answer Key

Page 13

Lesson 1.7 Least Common Multiple

The **least common multiple (LCM)** is the lowest multiple that a set of numbers has in common.

Find the least common multiple of 4, 6, and 9 by listing the multiples of each number until you find the first one that is shared.

$$4: 4, 8, 12, 16, 20, 24, 28, 32, 36$$
$$6: 6, 12, 18, 24, 30, 36$$
$$9: 9, 18, 27, 36$$

The LCM of 4, 6, and 9 is **36**.

What is a possible combination of 3 numbers with a LCM of 60?
List the factors of 60: 1, 2, 3, 4, 5, 6, 10, 12, 15, 20, 30, 60

Choose 3 of the factors:

2, 15, 30 is not a possible combination. Although they all have a common multiple of 60, the least common multiple is 30.

12, 15, 30 is a possible combination. Although 30 is a common multiple of 15 and 30, it is not a multiple of 12; therefore 60 is the least common multiple.

Give 2 sets of numbers that have 100 as the LCM.

Factors of 100: 1, 2, 4, 5, 10, 20, 25, 50, 100
Possible answers:
20, 25, 50
50, 100
Give 2 sets of numbers that have 40 as the LCM.

Factors of 40: 1, 2, 4, 5, 8, 10, 20, 40
Possible answers:
4, 5, 8
2, 8, 10

Page 14

Lesson 1.8 GCF in the Real World

Mrs. Rankin has a class of 18 boys and 12 girls. How many teams with equal numbers of girls and boys can be made for Field Day?

Mrs. Rankin needs to divide her class into smaller groups, so she needs to find the GCF of the numbers of girls and boys.

$$12: 1, 2, 3, 4, 6, 12 \qquad 18: 1, 2, 3, 6, 9, 18$$

The GCF is 6. Six groups made up of 2 girls and 3 boys can be made for Field Day.

Solve the problems.

Shawn is making treat bags for her friends. She has 24 lollipops, 36 pieces of chocolate candy, and 60 pieces of gum. What is the greatest number of bags she can make if she puts an equal amount of each kind of candy in each treat bag?

24: 1, 2, 3, 4, 6, 8, 12, 24
36: 1, 2, 3, 4, 6, 9, 12, 18, 36
60: 1, 2, 3, 4, 5, 6, 10, 12, 15, 20, 30, 60
GCF is 12. Shawn can make 12 treat bags with 2 lollipops, 3 chocolates candies, and 5 pieces of gum.

Joanie made 8 bedazzled vests in her sewing class for all of her cousins. Give 2 possible combinations of the number of buttons, zippers, and sparkly stickers that she used to make the vests. Explain your reasoning.

There are 8 groups. List of multiples:
8, 16, 24, 32, 40, 48, 56, 64, 72, 80
2 possible combinations:
8 buttons, 16 zippers, 40 sparkly stickers
16 buttons, 24 zippers, 48 sparkly stickers

Page 15

Lesson 1.9 LCM in the Real World

Mr. Adams is grilling hot dogs. Hot dog packs have 8 hot dogs. Hot dog bun packs have 10 buns. Mr. Adams wants to have the same number of buns as hot dogs. How many packs of each should he buy?

To solve, find the LCM of 8 and 10.

$$8: 8, 16, 24, 32, 40$$
$$10: 10, 20, 30, 40$$

The LCM of 8 and 10 is 40. Mr. Adams needs to buy 5 packs of hot dogs and 4 packs of hot dog buns so that he can make 40 hot dogs.

Solve the problems. Show your work.

Bob is building a fence with 6-foot sections of fencing. Wendy is building a fence with 8-foot sections of fencing. Leo is building a fence with 4-foot sections. How long are the fences the first time they are the same length?
4: 4, 8, 12, 16, 20, 24
6: 6, 12, 18, 24
8: 8, 16, 24
LCM is 24. The fences will be the same length at 24 feet.
Three science classes at different schools are studying the growth of plants. The class at Lincoln Middle School measures their plants every 5 days. The class at Hairston Middle School measures their plants every 6 days. The class at Jackson Middle School measures their plants every 9 days. On what day will all three classes measure their plants?
5: 5, 10, 15, 20, 25, 30, 35, 40, 45, 50, 55, 60, 65, 70, 75, 80, 85, 90
6: 6, 12, 18, 24, 30, 36, 42, 48, 54, 60, 66, 72, 78, 84, 90
9: 9, 18, 27, 36, 45, 54, 63, 72, 81, 90

LCM is 90. All three classes will measure their plants on the 90th day.

Page 16

Lesson 1.10 Multiplying Decimals

When multiplying decimals, use the same methods as you do for multiplying multi-digit whole numbers. Consider the place values when determining the final answer.

Sharla paid $4.78 per pound for 2.5 pounds of grapes. How much did she pay in total?

$$4.78 \cdot 100 \text{ to make a whole number}$$
$$\times 2.5 \cdot 10 \text{ to make a whole number}$$
$$11.95$$

$$
\begin{array}{r}
478 \\
\times 25 \\
\hline
2390 = 478 \cdot 5 \\
9560 = 478 \cdot 20 \\
\hline
11950 \div 100, \div 10 \text{ to get} \\
\text{original place values}
\end{array}
$$

She paid $11.95.

Solve the problem. Show your work.

The Robotics Club is buying supplies to build 12 robots. Each robot consists of 1 central processing unit, 6 body parts, and 1 speaker. The central processing unit costs $42.18. The body parts cost $5.79 each and the speaker costs $21.30.

There are 34 members in the Robotics Club, and each paid a $33.25 membership fee. If they use the membership fees to purchase the robots, will they have enough to purchase the 12 robots?

12 central processing units:
$$42.18 \cdot 100 = 4218$$
$$\times 12$$
$$\begin{array}{r} 4218 \\ \times 12 \\ \hline 8436 \\ 42180 \\ \hline 50616 \div 100 \end{array}$$
506.16

12 speakers:
$$21.30 \cdot 100 = 2130$$
$$\times 12$$
$$\begin{array}{r} 2130 \\ \times 12 \\ \hline 4260 \\ 21300 \\ \hline 25560 \div 100 \end{array}$$
255.60

6 parts needed for 12 robots, 72 parts:
$$5.79 \cdot 100 = 579$$
$$\begin{array}{r} 579 \\ \times 72 \\ \hline 1158 \\ 40530 \\ \hline 41688 \div 100 \end{array}$$
416.88

Total needed: 506.16 + 416.88 + 255.60 = 1178.64
Amount collected:
$$33.25 \cdot 100 = 3325$$
$$\begin{array}{r} 3325 \\ \times 34 \\ \hline 13300 \\ 99750 \\ \hline 113050 \div 100 \end{array}$$
1130.50
The team will be 1178.64 − 1130.50 = **$48.14 short**.

Answer Key

Page 17

NAME _____

Lesson 1.11 Dividing Decimals

When dividing decimals, use the same methods as you do for dividing multi-digit whole numbers. Consider the place values when determining the final answer.

Jasay is making ribbons to decorate for the school dance. She has a roll of ribbon that is 106.02 inches long. She needs to cut the ribbon into 3.42-inch pieces. How many ribbons will she have?

$3.42\overline{)106.02}$ Multiply the divisor by 100 to make a whole number. Multiply the dividend by the same number (100).

$$342\overline{)10602}$$
$$\begin{array}{r} 31 \\ \underline{-10260} = 342 \cdot 30 \\ 342 \\ \underline{-342} = 342 \cdot 1 \\ 0 \end{array}$$

Jasay can make 31 ribbons.

Solve the problem. Show your work.
Jeri is making cookies for a bake sale. She needs to figure out how many batches she can make with the ingredients that she already has. The recipe calls for 0.25 cups of sugar. She has 2.75 cups of sugar. The recipe calls for 0.4 teaspoons of oats. She has 2 teaspoons of oats. The recipe also calls for 1.6 cups of flour. She has 9.6 cups of flour. How many batches can she make? Explain your reasoning.

$2.75 \div 0.25$
$$\begin{array}{r} 11 \\ 25\overline{)275} \\ \underline{-25} \\ 25 \\ \underline{-25} \\ 0 \end{array}$$
Multiply divisor and dividend times 100.

$2 \div 0.4$
$$\begin{array}{r} 5 \\ 4\overline{)20} \\ \underline{-20} \\ 0 \end{array}$$
Multiply divisor and dividend times 10.

$9.6 \div 1.6$
$$\begin{array}{r} 6 \\ 16\overline{)96} \\ \underline{-96} \\ 0 \end{array}$$
Multiply divisor and dividend times 10.

Although Jeri has enough sugar to make 11 batches of cookies, she is limited by the oats. She only has enough oats to make 5 batches and enough flour to make 6 batches.

Spectrum Critical Thinking for Math
Grade 6

Lesson 1.11
Dividing Decimals
17

Page 18

NAME _____

💡 **Check What You Learned**

Number Systems and Operations

Complete the number sentences to reflect the given property.

1. Distributive property: $7(4 + 6) = \underline{28} + 42$

2. Associative property: $(12 \cdot \underline{29}) \cdot 15 = 12 \cdot (29 \cdot 15)$

3. Commutative property: $(14 \cdot 11) + (8 \cdot 19) = (\underline{8} \cdot 19) + (14 \cdot \underline{11})$

Use the distributive property to multiply.

4. $21 \cdot 49$ $49 (20 + 1)$
$980 + 49$
$1,029$

Solve the problems.

5. The school soccer team has 34 players. Each player will get a special T-shirt to wear on game days. The T-shirts cost $17 each. How much money will the team spend on T-shirts? Use an area model to solve.

	x30	x4
10	300	40	= 340
7	210	28	= + 238
			578

The team will spend $578.

6. Lucy can drive 57 miles in an hour. How far can Lucy drive in 4 hours? Write two number sentences to describe the scenario.

$57 \cdot 4 = ?$
$? \div 4 = 57$

Spectrum Critical Thinking for Math
Grade 6
18

Chapter 1
Check What You Learned

CHAPTER 1 POSTTEST

Page 19

NAME _____

💡 **Check What You Learned**

Number Systems and Operations

7. The new youth basketball league is giving out prizes to recruit new players. Every 12th person who signs up will receive a free basketball. Every 15th person will receive a coupon for $10 off some new basketball shoes. What is the number of the person who will receive both the basketball and the coupon for the shoes?

12, 24, 36, 48, ⑥⓪
15, 30, 45, ⑥⓪

The 60th person will get the basketball and coupon.

8. A yard of fabric costs $14.50. How much is 2.3 yards of fabric?

$$\begin{array}{r} 14.50 \\ \times 2.3 \\ \hline \mathbf{\$33.35} \end{array}$$
$\begin{array}{r} \cdot 100 \\ \cdot 10 \end{array}$
$$\begin{array}{r} 1450 \\ \times 23 \\ \hline 4350 \\ 29000 \\ \hline 33,350 \div 1000 \end{array}$$

9. Camilla's grandmother lives 23.6 miles away. Her best friend's grandmother lives 3.4 times farther away. How far away does her best friend's grandmother live?

$$\begin{array}{r} 23.6 \\ \times 3.4 \\ \hline \mathbf{80.24} \\ \textbf{miles} \end{array}$$
$\begin{array}{r} \cdot 10 \\ \cdot 10 \end{array}$
$$\begin{array}{r} 236 \\ \times 34 \\ \hline 944 \\ 7080 \\ \hline 8024 \div 100 \end{array}$$

Spectrum Critical Thinking for Math
Grade 6

Chapter 1
Check What You Learned
19

CHAPTER 1 POSTTEST

Page 20

NAME _____

CHAPTER 2 PRETEST

🔍 **Check What You Know**

Multiplying and Dividing Fractions

Solve the problems. Show your work.

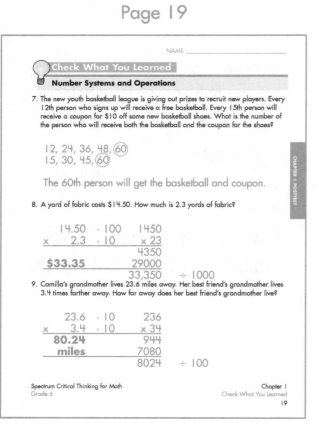

1. $\frac{3}{8} \cdot \frac{2}{3}$

$\frac{3}{8} \cdot \frac{2}{3} = \frac{6}{24} = \frac{1}{4}$

2. $6\frac{1}{3} \cdot 6$

$6\frac{1}{3} = \frac{19}{3}$

$\frac{19}{3} \cdot \frac{6}{1} = \frac{114}{3} = 38$

3. $2\frac{1}{2} \cdot 3\frac{3}{4}$

$2\frac{1}{2} = \frac{5}{2}$ $3\frac{3}{4} = \frac{15}{4}$

$\frac{5}{2} \cdot \frac{15}{4} = \frac{75}{8} = 9\frac{3}{8}$

4. $12 \div \frac{1}{3}$

$12 \div \frac{1}{3}$

$\frac{12}{1} \cdot \frac{3}{1} = \frac{36}{1} = 36$

5. $\frac{4}{5} \div \frac{3}{10}$

$\frac{4}{5} \div \frac{3}{10}$

$\frac{4}{5} \cdot \frac{10}{3} = \frac{40}{15} = 2\frac{10}{15} = 2\frac{2}{3}$

6. $2\frac{1}{3} \div 1\frac{1}{2}$

$2\frac{1}{3} = \frac{7}{3}$ $1\frac{1}{2} = \frac{3}{2}$

$\frac{7}{3} \div \frac{3}{2}$ $\frac{7}{3} \cdot \frac{2}{3} = \frac{14}{9} = 1\frac{5}{9}$

Spectrum Critical Thinking for Math
Grade 6
20

Chapter 2
Check What You Know

Page 21

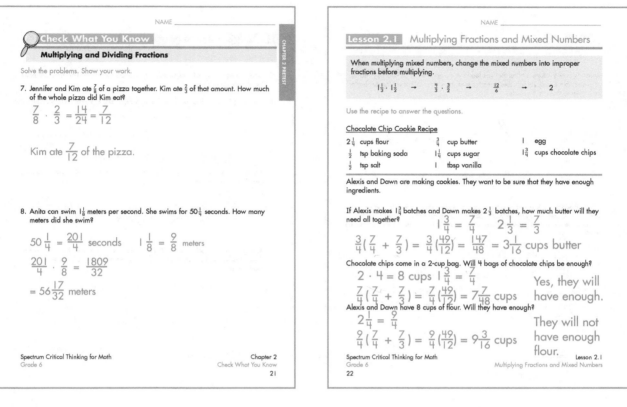

NAME _____

Check What You Know

Multiplying and Dividing Fractions

CHAPTER 2 PRETEST

Solve the problems. Show your work.

7. Jennifer and Kim ate $\frac{7}{8}$ of a pizza together. Kim ate $\frac{2}{3}$ of that amount. How much of the whole pizza did Kim eat?

$$\frac{7}{8} \cdot \frac{2}{3} = \frac{14}{24} = \frac{7}{12}$$

Kim ate $\frac{7}{12}$ of the pizza.

8. Anita can swim $1\frac{1}{8}$ meters per second. She swims for $50\frac{1}{4}$ seconds. How many meters did she swim?

$$50\frac{1}{4} = \frac{201}{4} \text{ seconds} \quad 1\frac{1}{8} = \frac{9}{8} \text{ meters}$$

$$\frac{201}{4} \cdot \frac{9}{8} = \frac{1809}{32}$$

$$= 56\frac{17}{32} \text{ meters}$$

Spectrum Critical Thinking for Math
Grade 6

Chapter 2
Check What You Know
21

Page 22

NAME _____

Lesson 2.1 Multiplying Fractions and Mixed Numbers

When multiplying mixed numbers, change the mixed numbers into improper fractions before multiplying.

$$1\frac{1}{3} \cdot 1\frac{1}{2} \quad \rightarrow \quad \frac{4}{3} \cdot \frac{3}{2} \quad \rightarrow \quad \frac{12}{6} \quad \rightarrow \quad 2$$

Use the recipe to answer the questions.

Chocolate Chip Cookie Recipe

$2\frac{1}{4}$ cups flour	$\frac{3}{4}$ cup butter	1 egg
$\frac{1}{2}$ tsp baking soda	$1\frac{1}{4}$ cups sugar	$1\frac{3}{4}$ cups chocolate chips
$\frac{1}{2}$ tsp salt	1 tbsp vanilla	

Alexis and Dawn are making cookies. They want to be sure that they have enough ingredients.

If Alexis makes $1\frac{3}{4}$ batches and Dawn makes $2\frac{1}{3}$ batches, how much butter will they need all together?

$$1\frac{3}{4} = \frac{7}{4} \qquad 2\frac{1}{3} = \frac{7}{3}$$

$$\frac{3}{4}\left(\frac{7}{4} + \frac{7}{3}\right) = \frac{3}{4}\left(\frac{49}{12}\right) = \frac{147}{48} = 3\frac{1}{16} \text{ cups butter}$$

Chocolate chips come in a 2-cup bag. Will 4 bags of chocolate chips be enough?

$$2 \cdot 4 = 8 \text{ cups} \quad 1\frac{3}{4} = \frac{7}{4}$$

$$\frac{7}{4}\left(\frac{7}{4} + \frac{7}{3}\right) = \frac{7}{4}\left(\frac{49}{12}\right) = 7\frac{7}{48} \text{ cups}$$

Yes, they will have enough.

Alexis and Dawn have 8 cups of flour. Will they have enough?

$$2\frac{1}{4} = \frac{9}{4}$$

$$\frac{9}{4}\left(\frac{7}{4} + \frac{7}{3}\right) = \frac{9}{4}\left(\frac{49}{12}\right) = 9\frac{3}{16} \text{ cups}$$

They will not have enough flour.

Spectrum Critical Thinking for Math
Grade 6
22

Lesson 2.1
Multiplying Fractions and Mixed Numbers

Page 23

NAME _____

Lesson 2.2 Dividing Fractions Using a Number Line

You can use a number line to divide fractions.

To solve $2\frac{1}{4} \div \frac{1}{2}$, note where $2\frac{1}{4}$ is on the number line. Starting at 0, count by $\frac{1}{2}$ until you reach $2\frac{1}{4}$. If you can't count by a full $\frac{1}{2}$, determine what fraction of $\frac{1}{2}$ will get you to $2\frac{1}{4}$.

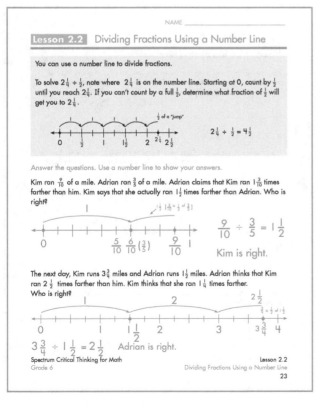

$$2\frac{1}{4} \div \frac{1}{2} = 4\frac{1}{2}$$

Answer the questions. Use a number line to show your answers.

Kim ran $\frac{9}{10}$ of a mile. Adrian ran $\frac{3}{5}$ of a mile. Adrian claims that Kim ran $1\frac{3}{10}$ times farther than him. Kim says that she actually ran $1\frac{1}{2}$ times farther than Adrian. Who is right?

$$\frac{9}{10} \div \frac{3}{5} = 1\frac{1}{2}$$

Kim is right.

The next day, Kim runs $3\frac{3}{4}$ miles and Adrian runs $1\frac{1}{2}$ miles. Adrian thinks that Kim ran $2\frac{1}{2}$ times farther than him. Kim thinks that she ran $1\frac{1}{4}$ times farther. Who is right?

$$3\frac{3}{4} \div 1\frac{1}{2} = 2\frac{1}{2} \quad \text{Adrian is right.}$$

Spectrum Critical Thinking for Math
Grade 6

Lesson 2.2
Dividing Fractions Using a Number Line
23

Page 24

NAME _____

Lesson 2.3 Dividing Mixed Numbers

You can divide mixed numbers by rewriting them as improper fractions and then multiplying the reciprocal of the divisor.

Sherri needs $5\frac{1}{4}$ inches of yarn to make a braided keychain. She found $16\frac{1}{2}$ inches of yarn in her room. How many keychains can she make?

$$16\frac{1}{2} \div 5\frac{1}{4} \quad \rightarrow \quad \frac{33}{2} \div \frac{21}{4} \quad \rightarrow \quad \frac{33}{2} \cdot \frac{4}{21} \quad \rightarrow \quad \frac{132}{42} = \frac{22}{7} = 3\frac{1}{7}$$

She can make $3\frac{1}{7}$ keychains.

Kevin is making decorations for the athletic banquet. To make each table centerpiece, he will need:

$1\frac{3}{4}$ inches white ribbon	$3\frac{2}{5}$ inches red ribbon
$2\frac{1}{8}$ inches blue ribbon	$4\frac{1}{4}$ inches green ribbon

Use the information above to solve this problem and the two problems on the next page.

Kevin found some leftover ribbon in a box. Assuming he had enough of the other colors needed, how many centerpieces can be made if he found $6\frac{1}{2}$ inches of white ribbon and $8\frac{1}{8}$ inches of blue ribbon?

$$6\frac{1}{2} = \frac{13}{2} \quad \frac{13}{2} \div \frac{7}{4} = \qquad 8\frac{1}{8} = \frac{65}{8} \quad \frac{65}{8} \div \frac{17}{8} =$$

$$\frac{13}{2} \cdot \frac{4}{7} = \frac{52}{14} = \frac{26}{7} = 3\frac{5}{7} \qquad \frac{65}{8} \cdot \frac{8}{17} = \frac{520}{136} = \frac{65}{17} = 3\frac{14}{17}$$

There is enough white ribbon and blue ribbon for 3.

Spectrum Critical Thinking for Math
Grade 6
24

Lesson 2.3
Dividing Mixed Numbers

Answer Key

Page 25

Lesson 2.3 Dividing Mixed Numbers

Solve the problems. Show your work.

Kimberly brought some ribbon that she found in the art room. She had $10\frac{5}{8}$ inches of green ribbon and $12\frac{7}{10}$ inches of red ribbon. How does this affect the number of centerpieces that can be made?

$10\frac{5}{8} = \frac{85}{8}$ $12\frac{7}{10} = \frac{127}{10}$

$\frac{85}{8} \div \frac{17}{4}$ $\frac{127}{10} \div \frac{17}{5}$

$\frac{85}{8} \cdot \frac{4}{17}$ $\frac{127}{10} \cdot \frac{5}{17}$

$\frac{5}{2} = 2\frac{1}{2}$ $\frac{127}{34} = 3\frac{25}{34}$

The green ribbon will allow them to make only 2 centerpieces.

Cheryl thought that it would be a good idea to add another color to the centerpiece. She wants to add $2\frac{1}{2}$ inches of yellow ribbon to each centerpiece. She brings $9\frac{1}{4}$ inches of yellow ribbon. How does this affect the number of centerpieces than can be made?

$9\frac{1}{4} = \frac{37}{4}$ $2\frac{1}{2} = \frac{5}{2}$

$\frac{37}{4} \div \frac{5}{2}$

$\frac{37}{4} \cdot \frac{2}{5}$

$\frac{37}{10} = 3\frac{7}{10}$

This is enough to make 3 centerpieces, but there still isn't enough green.

Page 26

Lesson 2.4 Mixed Numbers in the Real World

Solve the problems. Show your work.

Jim and Steve have started a fence-painting business for the summer. They can paint $3\frac{5}{8}$ feet of a fence in $1\frac{1}{2}$ hours.

1. If Jim and Steve worked for $5\frac{3}{8}$ hours, how many feet of fence did they paint?

$3\frac{5}{8} \div 1\frac{1}{2}$ = feet painted each hour

$\frac{29}{8} \div \frac{3}{2} = \frac{29}{8} \cdot \frac{2}{3} = \frac{29}{12} = 2\frac{5}{12}$ feet painted each hour

$2\frac{5}{12} \cdot 5\frac{3}{8} = \frac{29}{12} \cdot \frac{43}{8} = \frac{1247}{96} = 12\frac{95}{96}$ feet

2. The Johnsons have a fence that is $22\frac{3}{8}$ feet long. How long will it take for Jim and Steve to paint the fence?

$22\frac{3}{8} = \frac{179}{8}$

$\frac{179}{8} \div \frac{29}{12} = \frac{179}{8} \cdot \frac{12}{29} = \frac{2148}{232} = 9\frac{15}{58}$ hours

3. Steve got sick and could not help Jim paint the Johnsons' fence. When Jim paints alone, it takes him $1\frac{3}{4}$ hours to paint $1\frac{1}{4}$ feet of fence. How long will it take Jim to paint the fence alone?

$1\frac{3}{4} \div 1\frac{1}{4}$ = amount he can paint in 1 hour

$\frac{7}{4} \div \frac{5}{4} = \frac{7}{4} \cdot \frac{4}{5} =$ $\frac{179}{8} \div \frac{7}{5} = \frac{179}{8} \cdot \frac{5}{7}$

$\frac{7}{5}$ foot each hour $\frac{895}{56} = 15\frac{55}{56}$

Almost 16 hours

Page 27

💡 **Check What You Learned**

Multiplying and Dividing Fractions

1. Ahmad has $7\frac{1}{2}$ cups of trail mix. He wants to make $\frac{3}{4}$-cup servings for his friends. How many servings can he make? Use a number line to show your answer.

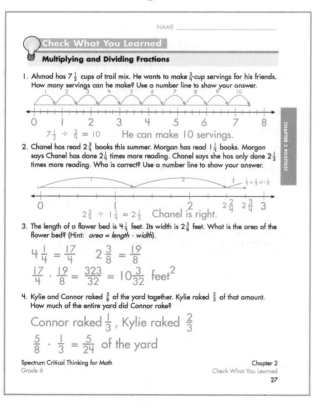

$7\frac{1}{2} \div \frac{3}{4} = 10$ He can make 10 servings.

2. Chanel has read $2\frac{3}{4}$ books this summer. Morgan has read $1\frac{1}{4}$ books. Morgan says Chanel has done $2\frac{1}{4}$ times more reading. Chanel says she has only done $2\frac{1}{5}$ times more reading. Who is correct? Use a number line to show your answer.

$2\frac{3}{4} \div 1\frac{1}{4} = 2\frac{1}{5}$ Chanel is right.

3. The length of a flower bed is $4\frac{1}{4}$ feet. Its width is $2\frac{3}{8}$ feet. What is the area of the flower bed? (Hint: *area = length · width*).

$4\frac{1}{4} = \frac{17}{4}$ $2\frac{3}{8} = \frac{19}{8}$

$\frac{17}{4} \cdot \frac{19}{8} = \frac{323}{32} = 10\frac{3}{32}$ feet^2

4. Kylie and Connor raked $\frac{5}{8}$ of the yard together. Kylie raked $\frac{2}{3}$ of that amount. How much of the entire yard did Connor rake?

Connor raked $\frac{1}{3}$, Kylie raked $\frac{2}{3}$

$\frac{5}{8} \cdot \frac{1}{3} = \frac{5}{24}$ of the yard

CHAPTER 2 POSTTEST

Page 28

💡 **Check What You Learned**

Multiplying and Dividing Fractions

CHAPTER 2 POSTTEST

5. Jacob drove $15\frac{1}{2}$ miles a day for 6 days in a row. How many miles would he have to drive a day to cover the same distance in $\frac{1}{3}$ the number of days?

$15\frac{1}{2} = \frac{31}{2}$ $\frac{1}{3} \cdot 6 = 2$ days

$\frac{31}{2} \cdot \frac{6}{1} = \frac{186}{2}$ $\frac{93}{2} = 46\frac{1}{2}$ miles per day

$= 93$ miles total

6. Marquise has $24\frac{1}{2}$ pounds of dog food. He feeds his dog $1\frac{3}{4}$ pounds twice a day. How many days will he be able to feed his dog before buying more dog food?

$1\frac{3}{4} = \frac{7}{4}$ $\frac{49}{2} \div \frac{7}{2}$

$\frac{7}{4} \cdot 2 = \frac{14}{4} = \frac{7}{2}$ $\frac{49}{2} \cdot \frac{2}{7} = 7$ days

$24\frac{1}{2} = \frac{49}{2}$ pounds of dog food

7. How many pieces of $\frac{5}{8}$-inch rope can be cut from a $3\frac{3}{4}$ inch rope?

$3\frac{3}{4} \div \frac{5}{8}$

$\frac{15}{4} \cdot \frac{8}{5} = 6$ pieces

8. Rochelle has $5\frac{2}{5}$ pounds of candy. Monica has $3\frac{2}{3}$ times as much candy. How much candy does she have?

$5\frac{2}{5} = \frac{27}{5}$ $3\frac{2}{3} = \frac{11}{3}$

$\frac{27}{5} \cdot \frac{11}{3} = \frac{297}{15} = 19\frac{12}{15} = 19\frac{4}{5}$ pounds

Page 29

NAME _____

Check What You Know

Ratios, Rates, and Percents

1. There are 4 girls for every 7 boys in the swim club. Complete the following table with equivalent ratios:

	×2	×3	×2
Girls	4	8	12	16
Boys	7	14	21	28
	×2	×3	×2

2. Lisa found a new recipe for punch. The punch contains 3 cups of pineapple juice for every 4 cups of orange juice. How many cups of orange juice must she use, if she uses 12 cups of pineapple juice?

×4

pineapple | 3 | 12   She must use 16
orange | 4 | 16   cups of orange juice.

×4

3. 3 tablespoons of sugar has 144 calories. Sugar has ___48___ calories per tablespoon.

$$\frac{144}{3} = \frac{48}{1}$$ ÷3 ÷3

4. Write $\frac{4}{5}$ as a decimal and a percent.

0.8   80%

Page 30

NAME _____

Check What You Know

Ratios, Rates, and Percents

5. Janet wants to make limeade punch for the party. She found two recipes. One of the recipes calls for 2 cups of lime juice for every 3 cups of water. The other recipe calls for 3 cups of lime juice for every 5 cups of water. Which limeade will have a stronger lime taste?

÷3   ÷5

$$\frac{2 \text{ lime}}{3 \text{ water}} = \frac{0.67}{1}$$ $$\frac{3 \text{ lime}}{5 \text{ water}} = \frac{0.6}{1}$$

÷3   ÷5

The first recipe is stronger because $\frac{2}{3} > \frac{3}{5}$

6. Which is the best buy?

	Size (oz.)	Price ($)
Regular Size Detergent	96	8.64
Family Size Detergent	128	10.24

Regular
$$\frac{8.64}{96} = \$0.09/\text{ounce}$$

Family
$$\frac{10.24}{128} = \$0.08/\text{ounce}$$

Family is the best buy.

7. Kenya bought a dress that usually costs $60, but she got a 35% discount. How much did she save?

×7   ÷20   She saved $21.

| 0% | 5% | | 35% | 50% | | 100% |
| 0 | 3 | | 21 | 30% | | 60 |

×7   ÷20

Page 31

NAME _____

Lesson 3.1 Comparing Ratios Using Ratio Tables

The table below represents the number of hours passed since Jorge posted a video on social media to raise awareness of endangered animal species in his state. He is tracking how many times the video was watched. How many views were there after 6 hours? After how many hours would there be 160 views?

×5
÷3

Hours	2	6	10
Views	32	96	160

÷3
×5

There were 96 views after 6 hours. After 10 hours, there were 160 views.

Use ratio tables to answer the questions.

A recipe calls for 7 cups of milk for every 21 cups of flour. If Chef Rachel puts in 147 cups of flour, how many cups of milk must she add?

×7

milk | 7 | 49   49 cups of milk
flour | 21 | 147

×7

Chef Rachel wants to make a smaller batch of the recipe and use only 1 cup of milk. How many cups of flour will she use?

÷7

milk | 7 | 1   3 cups of flour
flour | 21 | 3

÷7

Page 32

NAME _____

Lesson 3.2 Ratio Tables in the Real World

Students at Lyons Middle School are doing a service project. They are collecting footballs, basketballs, volleyballs, and soccer balls for local community centers. They have collected a total of 105 balls.

- The students collected twice as many footballs as volleyballs.
- They collected four times as many soccer balls as footballs.
- They collected three times as many basketballs as soccer balls.

Complete the ratio table to figure out how many balls of each type were collected.

× 2   × 3

Volleyballs	1	2	3
Footballs	2	4	6
Soccer Balls	8	16	24
Basketballs	24	48	72
Total	35	70	105

The students collected

___3___ volleyballs   ___6___ footballs

___24___ soccer balls   ___72___ basketballs

Answer Key

Page 33

NAME _____

Lesson 3.3 Comparing Ratios Using Unit Rates

Unit rates are useful when trying to compare two or more proportional relationships.

Sasha read 20 pages in 10 minutes. Brian read 12 pages in 4 minutes. Who read faster? How long would it take Brian to read a 104-page book?

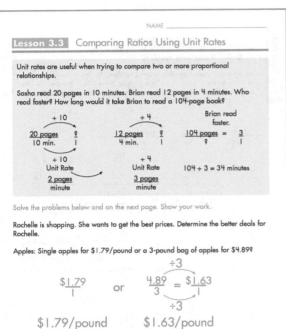

Solve the problems below and on the next page. Show your work.

Rochelle is shopping. She wants to get the best prices. Determine the better deals for Rochelle.

Apples: Single apples for $1.79/pound or a 3-pound bag of apples for $4.89?

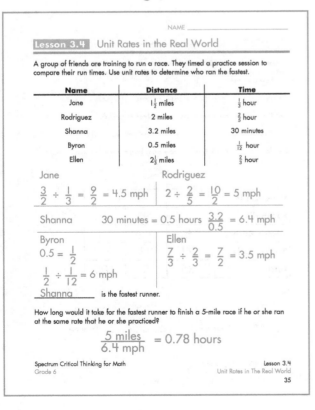

$$\frac{\$1.79}{1} \quad \text{or} \quad \frac{4.89}{3} \xrightarrow{\div 3} = \frac{\$1.63}{1}$$

$1.79/pound $1.63/pound

Bag of apples is a better deal.

Spectrum Critical Thinking for Math
Grade 6

Lesson 3.3
Comparing Ratios Using Unit Rates
33

Page 34

NAME _____

Lesson 3.3 Comparing Ratios Using Unit Rates

Cereal: 32-ounce box for $4.80 or 26-ounce box for $3.90?

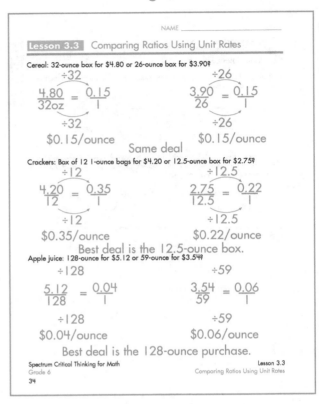

$$\frac{4.80}{32oz} \xrightarrow{\div 32} = \frac{0.15}{1} \qquad \frac{3.90}{26} \xrightarrow{\div 26} = \frac{0.15}{1}$$

$0.15/ounce $0.15/ounce

Same deal

Crackers: Box of 12 1-ounce bags for $4.20 or 12.5-ounce box for $2.75?

$$\frac{4.20}{12} \xrightarrow{\div 12} = \frac{0.35}{1} \qquad \frac{2.75}{12.5} \xrightarrow{\div 12.5} = \frac{0.22}{1}$$

$0.35/ounce $0.22/ounce

Best deal is the 12.5-ounce box.

Apple juice: 128-ounce for $5.12 or 59-ounce for $3.54?

$$\frac{5.12}{128} \xrightarrow{\div 128} = \frac{0.04}{1} \qquad \frac{3.54}{59} \xrightarrow{\div 59} = \frac{0.06}{1}$$

$0.04/ounce $0.06/ounce

Best deal is the 128-ounce purchase.

Spectrum Critical Thinking for Math
Grade 6

Lesson 3.3
Comparing Ratios Using Unit Rates
34

Page 35

NAME _____

Lesson 3.4 Unit Rates in the Real World

A group of friends are training to run a race. They timed a practice session to compare their run times. Use unit rates to determine who ran the fastest.

Name	Distance	Time
Jane	$1\frac{1}{2}$ miles	$\frac{1}{3}$ hour
Rodriguez	2 miles	$\frac{2}{5}$ hour
Shanna	3.2 miles	30 minutes
Byron	0.5 miles	$\frac{1}{12}$ hour
Ellen	$2\frac{1}{3}$ miles	$\frac{2}{3}$ hour

Jane

$$\frac{3}{2} \div \frac{1}{3} = \frac{9}{2} = 4.5 \text{ mph}$$

Rodriguez

$$2 \div \frac{2}{5} = \frac{10}{2} = 5 \text{ mph}$$

Shanna   30 minutes = 0.5 hours $\frac{3.2}{0.5} = 6.4$ mph

Byron

$$0.5 = \frac{1}{2}$$
$$\frac{1}{2} \div \frac{1}{12} = 6 \text{ mph}$$

Ellen

$$\frac{7}{3} \div \frac{2}{3} = \frac{7}{2} = 3.5 \text{ mph}$$

Shanna is the fastest runner.

How long would it take for the fastest runner to finish a 5-mile race if he or she ran at the same rate that he or she practiced?

$$\frac{5 \text{ miles}}{6.4 \text{ mph}} = 0.78 \text{ hours}$$

Spectrum Critical Thinking for Math
Grade 6

Lesson 3.4
Unit Rates in The Real World
35

Page 36

NAME _____

Lesson 3.5 Fractions, Decimals, and Percents

$\frac{25}{100}$ can also be written as twenty-five hundredths (0.25).

$\frac{4}{25}$ is equivalent to $\frac{16}{100}$. This can be written as 16 hundredths (0.16).

Percent means "per 100." $\frac{25}{100}$ is equivalent to 25%.

In 2013, the trash collected in Middleville included paper; yard waste and food; plastics; metals; rubber; leather; textiles; wood; glass; and other items.

Complete the table below that shows how much of each type of trash was collected.

	Fraction	Decimal	Percent
Paper	$\frac{27}{100}$	0.27	27%
Yard waste and food	$\frac{14}{50}$ $\frac{28}{100}$	0.28	28%
Plastics	$\frac{13}{100}$	0.13	13%
Metals	$\frac{9}{100}$	0.09	9%
Rubber, leather, and textiles	$\frac{9}{100}$	0.09	9%
Wood	$\frac{3}{50}$ $\frac{6}{100}$	0.06	6%
Glass	$\frac{1}{20}$ $\frac{5}{100}$	0.05	5%
Other	$\frac{3}{100}$	0.03	3%

Spectrum Critical Thinking for Math
Grade 6

Lesson 3.5
Fractions, Decimals, and Percents
36

Answer Key

Page 37

NAME

Lesson 3.6 Using a Bar Model to Find Percent

There are 30 students in Mr. Freeman's room. 40% of them are wearing shorts. How many students are wearing shorts?

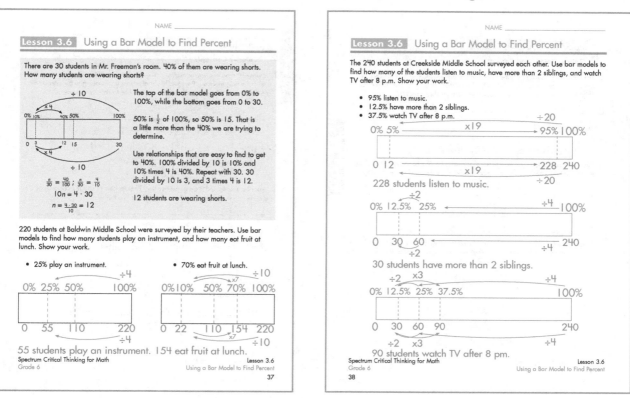

The top of the bar model goes from 0% to 100%, while the bottom goes from 0 to 30.

50% is $\frac{1}{2}$ of 100%, so 50% is 15. That is a little more than the 40% we are trying to determine.

Use relationships that are easy to find to get to 40%. 100% divided by 10 is 10% and 10% times 4 is 40%. Repeat with 30. 30 divided by 10 is 3, and 3 times 4 is 12.

$\frac{n}{30} = \frac{40}{100}$; $\frac{n}{30} = \frac{4}{10}$

$10n = 4 \cdot 30$

$n = \frac{4 \cdot 30}{10} = 12$

12 students are wearing shorts.

220 students at Baldwin Middle School were surveyed by their teachers. Use bar models to find how many students play an instrument, and how many eat fruit at lunch. Show your work.

- 25% play an instrument.
- 70% eat fruit at lunch.

55 students play an instrument.   154 eat fruit at lunch.

Spectrum Critical Thinking for Math
Grade 6

Lesson 3.6
Using a Bar Model to Find Percent
37

Page 38

NAME

Lesson 3.6 Using a Bar Model to Find Percent

The 240 students at Creekside Middle School surveyed each other. Use bar models to find how many of the students listen to music, have more than 2 siblings, and watch TV after 8 p.m. Show your work.

- 95% listen to music.
- 12.5% have more than 2 siblings.
- 37.5% watch TV after 8 p.m.

228 students listen to music.

30 students have more than 2 siblings.

90 students watch TV after 8 pm.

Spectrum Critical Thinking for Math
Grade 6
38

Lesson 3.6
Using a Bar Model to Find Percent

Page 39

NAME

Lesson 3.7 Percents in the Real World

Rochelle is at the store looking for the best prices. What is the best deal? Solve the problems and show your work.

Laundry detergent: $10.89 for 99 ounces, or $15.00 with 8% off for 138 ounces

$\frac{10.89}{99}$ = $0.11/ounce   0.08(15.00) = 1.20

$15.00 − $1.20 = $13.80

138 ounces is the best buy. $\frac{13.80}{138}$ = $0.10/ounce

Paper towels: $8.88 for 6 rolls of 74 sheets, or $18.00 for 12 rolls of 60 sheets at 20% off

6 rolls x 74 sheets = 444   12 rolls x 60 sheets = 720

$\frac{8.88}{444}$ = $0.02/sheet   0.2(18.00) = 3.60

$18.00 − $3.60 = $14.40

$\frac{14.40}{720}$ = $0.02/sheet

Same buy

Shampoo: 16.9 ounces for $10.14, or 34 ounces for $22.00 with 15% off

$\frac{10.14}{16.9}$ = 0.60/ounce   (0.15)(22.00) = 3.30

22.00 − 3.30 = 18.70

$\frac{18.70}{34}$ = 0.55/ounce

The sale item is the best buy.

Spectrum Critical Thinking for Math
Grade 6

Lesson 3.7
Percents in the Real World
39

Page 40

NAME

Check What You Learned

Ratios, Rates, and Percents

1. There are 4 counselors for every 22 students at the wilderness camp. Complete the following table with equivalent ratios:

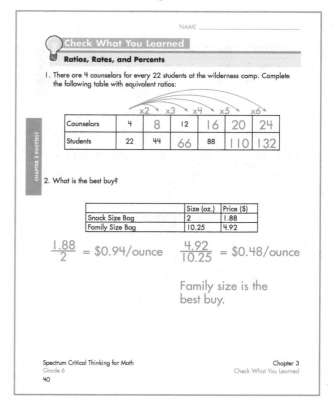

Counselors	4	8	12	16	20	24
Students	22	44	66	88	110	132

2. What is the best buy?

	Size (oz.)	Price ($)
Snack Size Bag	2	1.88
Family Size Bag	10.25	4.92

$\frac{1.88}{2}$ = $0.94/ounce $\frac{4.92}{10.25}$ = $0.48/ounce

Family size is the best buy.

CHAPTER 3 POSTTEST

Spectrum Critical Thinking for Math
Grade 6
40

Chapter 3
Check What You Learned

Answer Key

Page 41

NAME _____

Check What You Learned

Ratios, Rates, and Percents

3. The librarian is rearranging the books on the shelves. Now, 0.4 of the shelves are adult fiction, 38% of the shelves hold nonfiction, and $\frac{9}{20}$ of the shelves hold children's books. Which type of book uses the most shelf space?

$0.4 = 38\% = \frac{38}{100} = 0.38$ $\frac{9}{20} = \frac{45}{100} = 0.45 = 45\%$

$\frac{40}{100} = 40\%$

Children's books take up the most space.

4. Shanice is saving to buy a new jacket that costs $52. She has saved 45% of the money that she needs. How much more money does she need to save?

$$\begin{array}{r} 0.45 \\ \times\ 52 \\ \hline 23.40 \text{ saved} \end{array}$$

She needs 52 − 23.40 = $28.60 more.

5. Greta bought a television on sale for 20% off the original price. The original price was $60 more than the sale price. What was the original price of the television?

$$\frac{60}{?} = \frac{20}{100}$$

×3 ... ×3

$300

The TV was originally $300.

Page 42

NAME _____

Check What You Know

Integer Concepts

1. It was −4° F on one winter morning. The weather forecast said that it would be −8° F the next morning. Paul told his brother that it was going to be warmer the next morning. Was he right? Use the number line to show your answer.

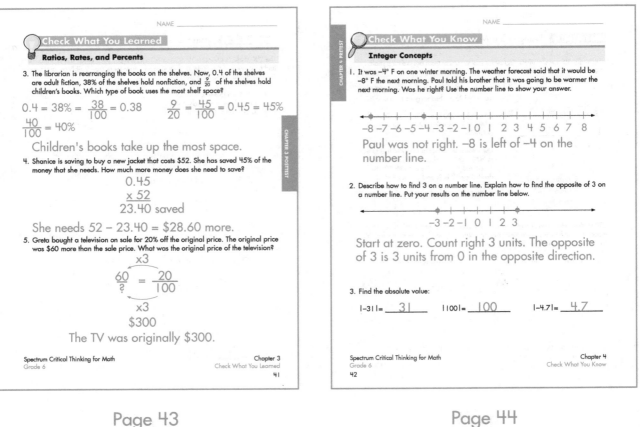

−8 −7 −6 −5 −4 −3 −2 −1 0 1 2 3 4 5 6 7 8

Paul was not right. −8 is left of −4 on the number line.

2. Describe how to find 3 on a number line. Explain how to find the opposite of 3 on a number line. Put your results on the number line below.

−3 −2 −1 0 1 2 3

Start at zero. Count right 3 units. The opposite of 3 is 3 units from 0 in the opposite direction.

3. Find the absolute value:

|−3| = __31__ |100| = __100__ |−4.7| = __4.7__

Page 43

NAME _____

Check What You Know

Integer Concepts

4. Write an integer to represent each real-world scenario.

a) A withdrawal of $200 __−200__   c) A $50 credit __+50__

b) 3 mph over the speed limit __+3__   d) 50 feet below sea level __−50__

5. The social studies class is making a map of the park. Graph and label the following coordinates on the coordinate plane:
Swing Set (−4, 3)   Slides (−3, −1)   Benches (−1, 1) & (−1, −1)
Picnic Tables (3,2)   Pond (5, −4)   Parking Lot (5, 4)

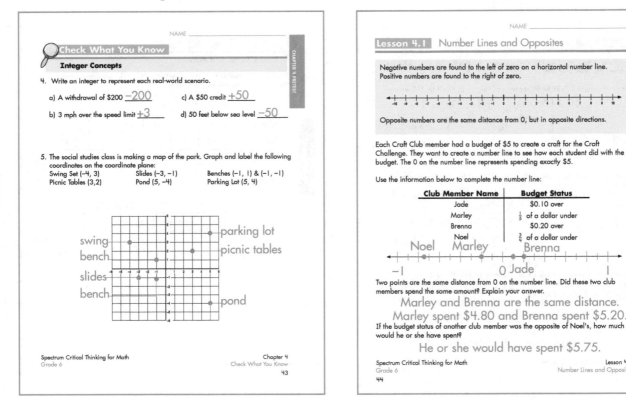

swing   parking lot
bench   picnic tables
slides
bench   pond

Page 44

NAME _____

Lesson 4.1 Number Lines and Opposites

Negative numbers are found to the left of zero on a horizontal number line. Positive numbers are found to the right of zero.

−10 −9 −8 −7 −6 −5 −4 −3 −2 −1 0 1 2 3 4 5 6 7 8 9 10

Opposite numbers are the same distance from 0, but in opposite directions.

Each Craft Club member had a budget of $5 to create a craft for the Craft Challenge. They want to create a number line to see how each student did with the budget. The 0 on the number line represents spending exactly $5.

Use the information below to complete the number line:

Club Member Name	Budget Status
Jade	$0.10 over
Marley	$\frac{1}{5}$ of a dollar under
Brenna	$0.20 over
Noel	$\frac{3}{4}$ of a dollar under

Noel   Marley   Brenna

−1   0 Jade   1

Two points are the same distance from 0 on the number line. Did these two club members spend the same amount? Explain your answer.

Marley and Brenna are the same distance. Marley spent $4.80 and Brenna spent $5.20.

If the budget status of another club member was the opposite of Noel's, how much would he or she have spent?

He or she would have spent $5.75.

Answer Key

Page 45

NAME

Lesson 4.2 Number Lines and Absolute Value

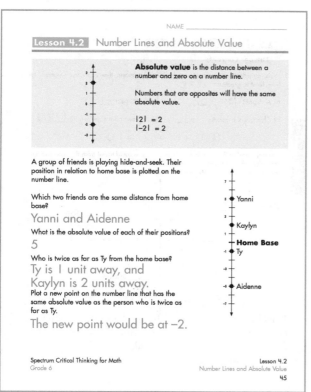

Absolute value is the distance between a number and zero on a number line.

Numbers that are opposites will have the same absolute value.

$|2| = 2$
$|-2| = 2$

A group of friends is playing hide-and-seek. Their position in relation to home base is plotted on the number line.

Which two friends are the same distance from home base?

Yanni and Aidenne

What is the absolute value of each of their positions?

5

Who is twice as far as Ty from the home base?

Ty is 1 unit away, and Kaylyn is 2 units away.

Plot a new point on the number line that has the same absolute value as the person who is twice as far as Ty.

The new point would be at −2.

Spectrum Critical Thinking for Math
Grade 6

Lesson 4.2
Number Lines and Absolute Value
45

Page 46

NAME

Lesson 4.3 Comparing and Ordering Integers

A group of students had a goal to eat 10 cups of fruits and vegetables daily. These numbers represent how far they were away from their goal:

$$-4.8, \frac{3}{2}, -5, 3.2$$

Put the numbers in order from least to greatest.

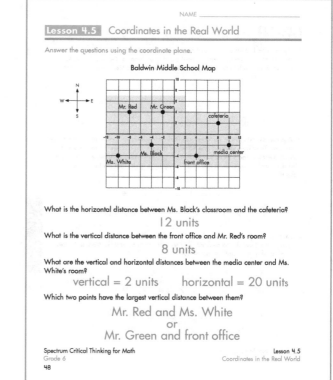

Least to greatest: $-5, -4.8, \frac{3}{2}, 3.2$

Dr. Williams is keeping track of how many cups of water her patients are drinking on average per day during the week. The goal is 8 cups of water. Use the information below to match the patient's name with the amount he or she drank. Zero means a patient drank exactly 8 cups of water a day.

Jewel	Sydney	Ayana	Kadrian	Derrick	Stacy	Misty	Wes
−7.2	$6\frac{1}{2}$	−3	−4.5	2	0	$10\frac{3}{4}$	$-6\frac{1}{2}$

Jewel drank the least amount of water. -7.2

Misty drank the most amount of water. $10\frac{3}{4}$

Derrick drank more than Stacy, but less than Sydney. $2, 6\frac{1}{2}$

Wes and Sydney are the same distance from the 8-cup goal. $6\frac{1}{2}$ and $-6\frac{1}{2}$

Stacy drank the recommended amount of water each day. 0

Kadrian didn't drink as much as Ayana. $-4.5, -3$

Spectrum Critical Thinking for Math
Grade 6
46

Lesson 4.3
Comparing and Ordering Integers

Page 47

NAME

Lesson 4.4 Integers in the Coordinate Plane

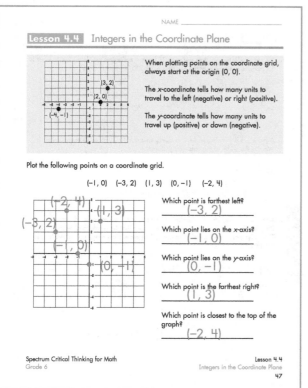

When plotting points on the coordinate grid, always start at the origin (0, 0).

The x-coordinate tells how many units to travel to the left (negative) or right (positive).

The y-coordinate tells how many units to travel up (positive) or down (negative).

Plot the following points on a coordinate grid.

$(-1, 0)$ $(-3, 2)$ $(1, 3)$ $(0, -1)$ $(-2, 4)$

Which point is farthest left?
$(-3, 2)$

Which point lies on the x-axis?
$(-1, 0)$

Which point lies on the y-axis?
$(0, -1)$

Which point is the farthest right?
$(1, 3)$

Which point is closest to the top of the graph?
$(-2, 4)$

Spectrum Critical Thinking for Math
Grade 6

Lesson 4.4
Integers in the Coordinate Plane
47

Page 48

NAME

Lesson 4.5 Coordinates in the Real World

Answer the questions using the coordinate plane.

Baldwin Middle School Map

What is the horizontal distance between Ms. Black's classroom and the cafeteria?
12 units

What is the vertical distance between the front office and Mr. Red's room?
8 units

What are the vertical and horizontal distances between the media center and Ms. White's room?
vertical = 2 units   horizontal = 20 units

Which two points have the largest vertical distance between them?
Mr. Red and Ms. White
or
Mr. Green and front office

Spectrum Critical Thinking for Math
Grade 6
48

Lesson 4.5
Coordinates in the Real World

Answer Key

Page 49

💡 Check What You Learned

Integer Concepts

1. Jacob said his account balance was −$20. Ed said his account balance was −$15. Jacob thinks his account is worth more than Ed's account. Ed thinks his account is worth more than Jacob's. Who is right? Use a number line to show your answer.

Jacob   Ed
−21 −20 −19 −18 −17 −16 −15 −14

Ed is right because −15 is to the right of −20.

2. If zero lies between w and z, give a possible set of values for w, x, y, and z.

w   x   y   z

Answers will vary. Possible answers:
$w = -6 \quad x = -2 \quad y = 2 \quad z = 6$

3. The melting point of hydrogen is −259°C. The melting point of sodium is about 98°C. Which temperature has the lowest absolute value?

$|-259| = 259 \qquad |98| = 98$

Sodium's temperature has the lowest absolute value.

4. At the start of the day, there were 30 students in the classroom. That number grew and shrank throughout the day. The integers 4, −1, −2, and 0 represent the change in the number of students in the classroom. List the integers in order from least to greatest. Explain the meaning of zero in this situation.

$-2 \quad -1 \quad 0 \quad 4$

Zero represents the number of students at the start of the day.

CHAPTER 4 POSTTEST

Page 50

💡 Check What You Learned

Integer Concepts

CHAPTER 4 POSTTEST

5. Write an integer to represent each real-world scenario, then order the integers from least to greatest.

a) A deposit of $52 $+52$ c) A $100 debt -100

b) Club gains 1 member $+1$ d) 1,000 feet above sea level $+1,000$

$-100 \quad +1 \quad +52 \quad +1,000$

6. Using the grid of the town below, show how you could travel from the school to the gym along the grid lines. Each unit represents $\frac{1}{2}$ mile. Use units and direction in your answer. You may only change direction once.

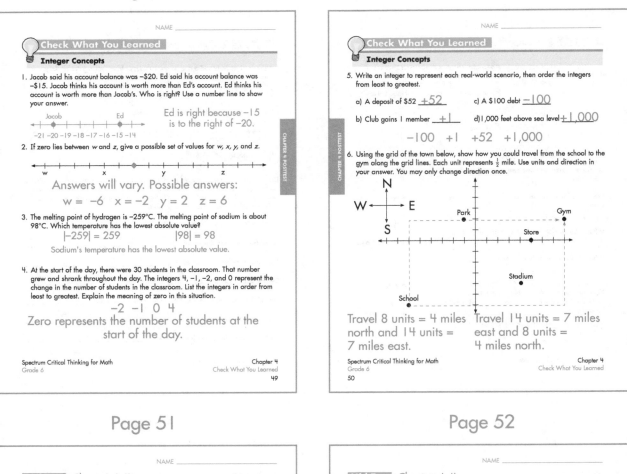

Travel 8 units = 4 miles north and 14 units = 7 miles east.

Travel 14 units = 7 miles east and 8 units = 4 miles north.

Page 51

Mid-Test Chapters 1–4

CHAPTERS 1–4 MID-TEST

1. During their last vacation, the McCoy family spent $515.72 in 4 days on food. They want to spend the same amount per day on food for this year's vacation. This year, they will take a 6-day vacation. What will be their total food cost?

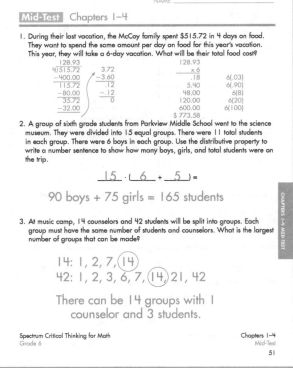

$$128.93$$
$$4)\overline{515.72}$$
$$-400.00$$
$$115.72$$
$$-80.00$$
$$35.72$$
$$-32.00$$

3.72
−3.60
.12
−.12
0

128.93
× 6
.18   6(.03)
5.40   6(.90)
48.00   6(8)
120.00   6(20)
600.00   6(100)
$ 773.58

2. A group of sixth grade students from Parkview Middle School went to the science museum. They were divided into 15 equal groups. There were 11 total students in each group. There were 6 boys in each group. Use the distributive property to write a number sentence to show how many boys, girls, and total students were on the trip.

$\underline{15} \cdot (\underline{6} + \underline{5}) =$

90 boys + 75 girls = 165 students

3. At music camp, 14 counselors and 42 students will be split into groups. Each group must have the same number of students and counselors. What is the largest number of groups that can be made?

14: 1, 2, 7, (14)
42: 1, 2, 3, 6, 7, (14), 21, 42

There can be 14 groups with 1 counselor and 3 students.

Page 52

Mid-Test Chapters 1–4

CHAPTERS 1–4 MID-TEST

4. Tara has collected 45 state quarters. If $\frac{2}{5}$ of her collection are dated 2007, what is the approximate value of the quarters from 2007?

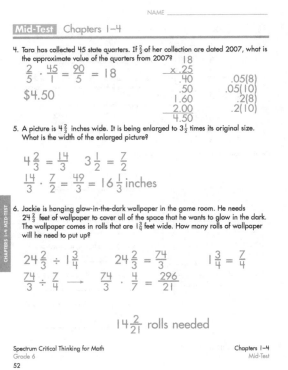

$$\frac{2}{5} \cdot \frac{45}{1} = \frac{90}{5} = 18$$

$$\$4.50$$

18
× .25
.40   .05(8)
.50   .05(10)
1.60   .2(8)
2.00   .2(10)
4.50

5. A picture is $4\frac{2}{3}$ inches wide. It is being enlarged to $3\frac{1}{2}$ times its original size. What is the width of the enlarged picture?

$$4\frac{2}{3} = \frac{14}{3} \qquad 3\frac{1}{2} = \frac{7}{2}$$

$$\frac{14}{3} \cdot \frac{7}{2} = \frac{49}{3} = 16\frac{1}{3} \text{ inches}$$

6. Jackie is hanging glow-in-the-dark wallpaper in the game room. He needs $24\frac{2}{3}$ feet of wallpaper to cover all of the space that he wants to glow in the dark. The wallpaper comes in rolls that are $1\frac{3}{4}$ feet wide. How many rolls of wallpaper will he need to put up?

$$24\frac{2}{3} \div 1\frac{3}{4} \qquad 24\frac{2}{3} = \frac{74}{3} \qquad 1\frac{3}{4} = \frac{7}{4}$$

$$\frac{74}{3} \div \frac{7}{4} \longrightarrow \frac{74}{3} \cdot \frac{4}{7} = \frac{296}{21}$$

$$14\frac{2}{21} \text{ rolls needed}$$

Page 53

Mid-Test Chapters 1–4

7. The ratio of black to white marbles in a bag is 3:4. If you take out 3 black marbles and 6 white ones, the ratio is 6:7. How many white marbles were originally in the bag?

b	3
w	4

$\dfrac{6-3}{8-6} = \dfrac{3}{2}$ NO

$\dfrac{12-3}{16-6} = \dfrac{9}{10}$ NO Test each equivalent ratio.

$\dfrac{15-3}{20-6} = \dfrac{12}{14} = \dfrac{6}{7}$ YES

$\dfrac{9-3}{12-6} = \dfrac{6}{6}$ NO

There were 20 white marbles.

8. A bus was traveling 70 feet per second. How many miles will the bus travel in 2.4 hours if it drives the same speed the entire time? Round to the nearest tenth. There are 5,280 feet in one mile.

$\dfrac{70 \text{ feet}}{\text{sec.}} \cdot \dfrac{60 \text{ sec}}{\text{min.}} = \dfrac{4200 \text{ feet}}{\text{min.}}$ $\dfrac{252000 \text{ ft./hr.}}{5280 \text{ ft./mile}} = 47.7$ mph

$\dfrac{4200 \text{ feet}}{\text{min.}} \cdot \dfrac{60 \text{ min}}{\text{hr.}} = \dfrac{252,000 \text{ feet}}{\text{hour}}$ 47.7 mph · 2.4 hrs = 114.5 miles

9. Graph each fraction, percent, or decimal on the number line.

$\dfrac{3}{5}$ 25% $\dfrac{60}{200}$ 0.15   90%

0.15 25% $\dfrac{60}{200}$ $\dfrac{3}{5}$ 90%

10. Sherry bought a shirt that was on sale for 20% off. She had a student discount card, so she got an additional 10% off the sale price. If the original price of the shirt was $25, how much did she pay for the shirt?

0.2 · 25 = $5 off
25 – 5 = $20
0.1(20) = $2 off
20 – 2 = $18

She paid $18 for the shirt.

Page 54

Mid-Test Chapters 1–4

11. The table shows points earned for each action in a video game. Assume that Justice started with zero points. Use a number line to determine his final score if he found a hidden treasure, reached a dead end, found a secret passage, climbed a magic staircase, and then got caught in a trap.

Action	Points
Climb a magic staircase	+3
Find a secret passage	+6
Find a hidden treasure	+9
Reach a dead end	–3
Get caught in a trap	–9

Justice's final score was 6 points.

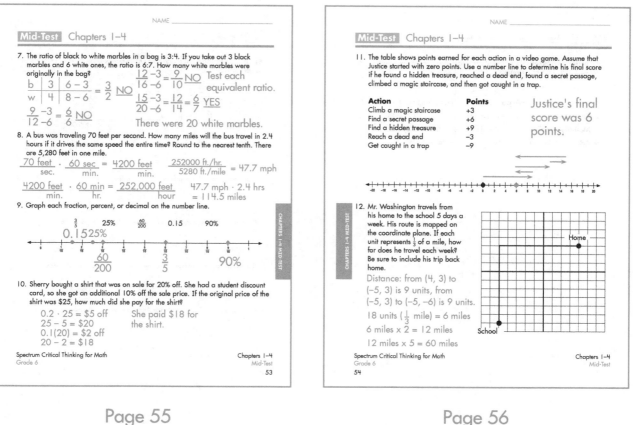

12. Mr. Washington travels from his home to the school 5 days a week. His route is mapped on the coordinate plane. If each unit represents $\frac{1}{3}$ of a mile, how far does he travel each week? Be sure to include his trip back home.

Distance: from (4, 3) to (–5, 3) is 9 units, from (–5, 3) to (–5, –6) is 9 units.

18 units ($\frac{1}{3}$ mile) = 6 miles

6 miles x 2 = 12 miles

12 miles x 5 = 60 miles

Page 55

Check What You Know

Expressions and Equations

1. Rewrite as a product: $4^4 =$ 4 · 4 · 4 · 4

   $\left(\frac{1}{2}\right)^3 =$ $\dfrac{1}{2} \cdot \dfrac{1}{2} \cdot \dfrac{1}{2}$

2. Rewrite using exponents: $11 \cdot 11 \cdot 11 \cdot 11 \cdot 11 =$ 11^5

   $7 \cdot 7 \cdot 7 =$ 7^3

3. Write using scientific notation: 80,000 = 8×10^4

4. Evaluate the expression: $2 \cdot 4^2 + 3(5 + 1) \div 6 =$ $2 \cdot 4^2 + 3(6) \div 6$
   $2 \cdot 16 + 18 \div 6$
   $32 + 18 \div 6$
   $32 + 3$
   $= 35$

5. Write each phrase as an algebraic expression:

   a. 10 less than x
   $x - 10$

   b. k represents Kayla's test grade. She made 10 points higher on her 2nd test.
   $k + 10$

   c. The product of 7 and m
   $7m$

6. Write an equivalent expression for each:

   $3(x + 7)$ $3x + 21$ $4x + x + 2x$ $7x$

7. What is the **6** in the expression $6x$? coefficient

Page 56

Check What You Know

Expressions and Equations

8. Solve for x: $x + 5 = 27$

$$\begin{array}{r} x + 5 = 27 \\ -5 \quad -5 \\ \hline x = 22 \end{array}$$

9. Solve for x: $y - 7 > 27$

$$\begin{array}{r} y - 7 > 27 \\ +7 \quad +7 \\ \hline y > 34 \end{array}$$

10. Solve for x: $7x = 35$

$$\dfrac{7x}{7} = \dfrac{35}{7}$$
$$x = 5$$

11. Solve for x: $\frac{x}{3} \le 15$

$$\dfrac{x}{3} \le 15$$
$$3 \cdot \dfrac{x}{3} \le 15 \cdot 3$$
$$x \le 45$$

13. Tamar is two years older than Zane.

t = Tamar's age z = Zane's age

_z_ is the independent variable.

_t_ is the dependent variable.

Write an equation to describe the relationship.

$t = z + 2$

Answer Key

Page 57

Lesson 5.1 Order of Operations

The **order of operations** is a set of rules used to simplify numeric expressions that have more than one operation.

$(10 + 15) \div 5 + 2^2$

1. Perform operations within **parentheses**. $(25) \div 5 + 2^2$ **(10 + 15 = 25)**
2. Find values of numbers with **exponents**. $25 \div 5 + 4$ **(2^2 = 4)**
3. **Multiply** and **divide** from left to right. $5 + 4$ **(25 ÷ 5 = 5)**
4. **Add** and **subtract** from left to right. 9 **(5 + 4 = 9)**

Solve the problems using the order of operations. Show your work.

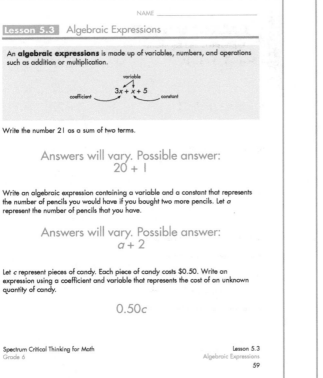

$7^2 - (4 + 2 \cdot 2) \cdot 6$

$7^2 - (4 + 4) \cdot 6$
$7^2 - 8 \cdot 6$
$49 - 8 \cdot 6$
$49 - 48$
①

$96 - 6 + 16 \div 4^2$

$96 - 6 + 16 \div 4^2$
$96 - 6 + 16 \div 16$
$96 - 6 + 1$
$90 + 1$
91

$(35 \div 5) \cdot 4 - 6 + 2^3$

$(35 \div 5) \cdot 4 - 6 + 2^3$
$7 \cdot 4 - 6 + 2^3$
$7 \cdot 4 - 6 + 8$
$28 - 6 + 8$
$22 + 8$
30

Page 58

Lesson 5.2 Scientific Notation

Scientific notation is a shortcut way to write very large numbers using the powers of 10.

10^2	$10 \cdot 10$	100
10^3	$10 \cdot 10 \cdot 10$	1,000
10^4	$10 \cdot 10 \cdot 10 \cdot 10$	10,000
10^5	$10 \cdot 10 \cdot 10 \cdot 10 \cdot 10$	100,000
10^6	$10 \cdot 10 \cdot 10 \cdot 10 \cdot 10 \cdot 10$	1,000,000

$40,000 = 4 \cdot 10,000 = 4 \times 10^4$

Write the following values using scientific notation.

1. The speed of sound is approximately 800 miles per hour.

$$800 = 8 \times 100 = 8 \times 10^2$$

2. The state of Colorado covers approximately 100,000 square miles.

$$100,000 = 1 \times 100,000 = 1 \times 10^5$$

3. The cost to attend Princeton University is approximately $60,000 per year.

$$60,000 = 6 \times 10,000 = 6 \times 10^4$$

4. The distance from New York to Los Angeles is over 2,000 miles.

$$2,000 = 2 \times 1,000 = 2 \times 10^3$$

Page 59

Lesson 5.3 Algebraic Expressions

An **algebraic expressions** is made up of variables, numbers, and operations such as addition or multiplication.

variable
coefficient $3x + x + 5$ constant

Write the number 21 as a sum of two terms.

Answers will vary. Possible answer:
$20 + 1$

Write an algebraic expression containing a variable and a constant that represents the number of pencils you would have if you bought two more pencils. Let a represent the number of pencils that you have.

Answers will vary. Possible answer:
$a + 2$

Let c represent pieces of candy. Each piece of candy costs $0.50. Write an expression using a coefficient and variable that represents the cost of an unknown quantity of candy.

$0.50c$

Page 60

Lesson 5.4 Expressions and Equations in the Real World

Expressions are made up of terms.

Mario had some apps on his smart phone. He deleted 3 apps.
This can be shown with the expression $a - 3$, where a = the number of apps.

Equations are expressions that have an equal sign (=).

Louis had 3 times as many apps as Mario until he downloaded 4 more apps.
This can be shown with the equation $l = 3m + 4$, where l = the number of apps that Louis has, and m = the number of apps that Mario has.

Write an expression or equation to represent each real-world scenario.

A teacher brings bookmarks for her students. She wants to give an equal number to each student. How many will she give to each student?

$$\frac{b}{s}$$

Rita needs 6 more shirts than the ones she already has. How many shirts does she need in all?

$$x + 6$$

Joe builds cornhole games. He takes 4 hours to make each game. Joe worked on creating games for 36 hours last week. How many cornhole games did he build?

$$\frac{36}{4} = x$$

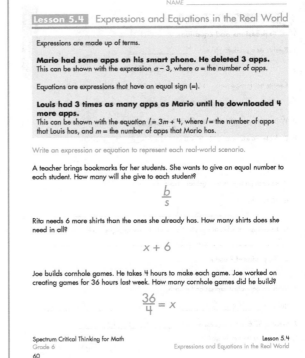

Answer Key

Page 61

NAME _____

Lesson 5.5 Writing Equivalent Expressions

The commutative and associative properties allow us to rewrite algebraic expressions in order to solve problems.

Amani has two sisters, Starr and Brianna. Starr is 1 year older than Amani. Brianna is 4 years older than Amani. What is the sum of the three sisters' ages?

The age of each person can be represented by an algebraic expression:
Amani: x Starr: $x + 1$ Brianna: $x + 4$

The sum of each person's age can be represented by the algebraic expression:
$x + (x + 1) + (x + 4)$

We can use the commutative and associative properties of addition to change the order and the grouping to rewrite the expression:
$(x + x + x) + (1 + 4)$

We can combine like terms to write the expression in simplest form:
$3x + 5$

The sum of their ages is $3x + 5$.

Use the commutative and associative properties to simplify the following expression:
$(8x + 9) + (7x + 4)$

$8x + 9 + 7x + 4$
$(8x + 7x) + (9 + 4)$
$= 15x + 13$

How would the simplified expression change if you added $2x + 1$ to the expression in the first problem?

$$\begin{array}{r} 15x + 13 \\ + \ 2x + \ 1 \\ \hline 17x + 14 \end{array}$$

Spectrum Critical Thinking for Math
Grade 6

Lesson 5.5
Writing Equivalent Expressions
61

Page 62

NAME _____

Lesson 5.5 Writing Equivalent Expressions

Solve the problems. Show your work.

Todd and his friends are buying school supplies. They needed folders to organize their school work. Folders can be purchased individually or in packs. Todd bought 1 pack of folders and 2 individual folders. Max bought 2 packs of folders and 1 individual folder. Zane bought 4 packs of folders and 3 individual folders. Write an expression in simplest form to represent the total number of folders bought. How many folders are in a pack if Todd and his friends bought a total of 41 folders?

Todd = 1 pack + 2
Max = 2 packs + 1
Zane = 4 packs + 3

$(p + 2) + (2p + 1) + (4p + 3)$ $(p + 2p + 4p) + (2 + 1 + 3)$
$7p + 6$
Guess and check:
$7(2) + 6 = 20$
$7(4) + 6 = 34$
$7(5) + 6 = 41$

There would be 5 folders in a pack.

Ms. Arberg is shopping for uniforms for the 11 players on her volleyball team. Adams' Print Shop has jerseys for j dollars and will add a number and a logo for $3. The shorts they offer cost s dollars plus $2 for the logo. Write an expression that tells how much the uniforms will cost.

$$11(j + 3) + 11(s + 2)$$

If the jerseys cost $12 without the number and logo and the shorts cost $7 without the logo, what is the total cost?

$$11(12 + 3) + 11(7 + 2)$$
$$= 11(15) + 11(9)$$
$$= 165 + 99$$
$$= \$264$$

Spectrum Critical Thinking for Math
Grade 6
62

Lesson 5.5
Writing Equivalent Expressions

Page 63

NAME _____

Lesson 5.6 Addition and Subtraction Equations

You can solve addition and subtraction equations using tape diagrams. Tape diagrams use rectangles to show different parts of an equation.

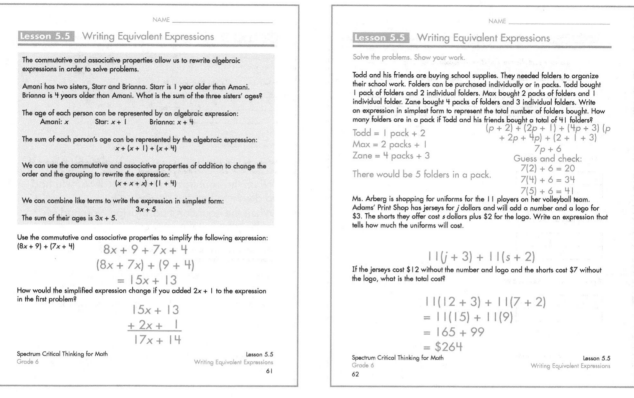

Write an equation for each description. Solve the equation using a tape diagram.

What number added to 7 is 21?

x	7
21	

$x + 7 = 21$

$21 - 7 = x$
$x = 14$

14 subtracted from what number is 7?

7	14
x	

$x - 14 = 7$

$7 + 14 = x$
$x = 21$

13 added to what number is 27?

x	13
27	

$x + 13 = 27$

$x = 27 - 13$
$x = 14$

Spectrum Critical Thinking for Math
Grade 6

Lesson 5.6
Addition and Subtraction Equations
63

Page 64

NAME _____

Lesson 5.6 Addition and Subtraction Equations

Write an equation for the description. Solve the equation using a tape diagram. Show your work.

14 fewer than a number is 13.

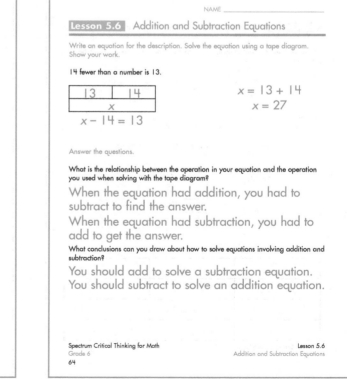

13	14
x	

$x - 14 = 13$

$x = 13 + 14$
$x = 27$

Answer the questions.

What is the relationship between the operation in your equation and the operation you used when solving with the tape diagram?

When the equation had addition, you had to subtract to find the answer.

When the equation had subtraction, you had to add to get the answer.

What conclusions can you draw about how to solve equations involving addition and subtraction?

You should add to solve a subtraction equation.

You should subtract to solve an addition equation.

Spectrum Critical Thinking for Math
Grade 6
64

Lesson 5.6
Addition and Subtraction Equations

Answer Key

Page 65

NAME _____

Lesson 5.7 Solving Multiplication and Division Equations

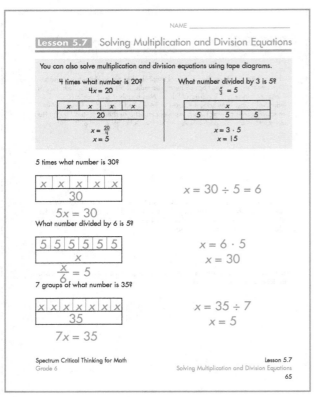

You can also solve multiplication and division equations using tape diagrams.

4 times what number is 20?
$4x = 20$

$x = \frac{20}{4}$
$x = 5$

What number divided by 3 is 5?
$\frac{x}{3} = 5$

$x = 3 \cdot 5$
$x = 15$

5 times what number is 30?

$x = 30 \div 5 = 6$

$5x = 30$

What number divided by 6 is 5?

$x = 6 \cdot 5$
$x = 30$

$\frac{x}{6} = 5$

7 groups of what number is 35?

$x = 35 \div 7$
$x = 5$

$7x = 35$

Page 66

NAME _____

Lesson 5.7 Solving Multiplication and Division Equations

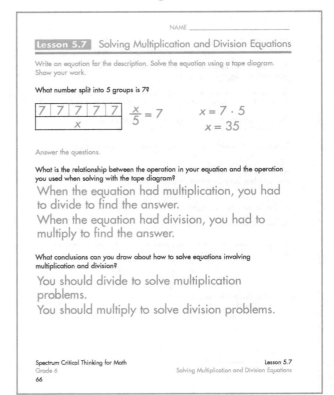

Write an equation for the description. Solve the equation using a tape diagram. Show your work.

What number split into 5 groups is 7?

$\frac{x}{5} = 7$

$x = 7 \cdot 5$
$x = 35$

Answer the questions.

What is the relationship between the operation in your equation and the operation you used when solving with the tape diagram?

When the equation had multiplication, you had to divide to find the answer.
When the equation had division, you had to multiply to find the answer.

What conclusions can you draw about how to solve equations involving multiplication and division?

You should divide to solve multiplication problems.
You should multiply to solve division problems.

Page 67

NAME _____

Lesson 5.8 Identifying Equivalent Equations

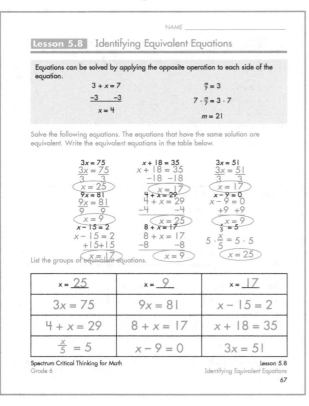

Equations can be solved by applying the opposite operation to each side of the equation.

$3 + x = 7$
$\underline{-3 \quad -3}$
$x = 4$

$\frac{m}{7} = 3$
$7 \cdot \frac{m}{7} = 3 \cdot 7$
$m = 21$

Solve the following equations. The equations that have the same solution are equivalent. Write the equivalent equations in the table below.

$3x = 75$
$\frac{3x}{3} = \frac{75}{3}$
$\boxed{x = 25}$
$9x = 81$
$\frac{9x}{9} = \frac{81}{9}$
$\boxed{x = 9}$
$x - 15 = 2$
$+15 +15$
$\boxed{x = 17}$

$x + 18 = 35$
$x + 18 = 35$
$-18 \quad -18$
$\boxed{x = 17}$
$4 + x = 29$
$4 + x = 29$
$-4 \quad -4$
$\boxed{x = 25}$
$8 + x = 17$
$8 + x = 17$
$-8 \quad -8$
$\boxed{x = 9}$

$3x = 51$
$\frac{3x}{3} = \frac{51}{3}$
$\boxed{x = 17}$
$x - 9 = 0$
$x - 9 = 0$
$+9 \quad +9$
$\boxed{x = 9}$
$\frac{x}{5} = 5$
$5 \cdot \frac{x}{5} = 5 \cdot 5$
$\boxed{x = 25}$

List the groups of equivalent equations.

$x = 25$	$x = 9$	$x = 17$
$3x = 75$	$9x = 81$	$x - 15 = 2$
$4 + x = 29$	$8 + x = 17$	$x + 18 = 35$
$\frac{x}{5} = 5$	$x - 9 = 0$	$3x = 51$

Page 68

NAME _____

Lesson 5.9 Solving Inequalities in the Real World

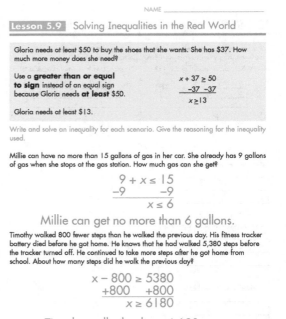

Gloria needs at least $50 to buy the shoes that she wants. She has $37. How much more money does she need?

Use a **greater than or equal to sign** instead of an equal sign because Gloria needs **at least** $50.

$x + 37 \geq 50$
$-37 \quad -37$
$x \geq 13$

Gloria needs at least $13.

Write and solve an inequality for each scenario. Give the reasoning for the inequality used.

Millie can have no more than 15 gallons of gas in her car. She already has 9 gallons of gas when she stops at the gas station. How much gas can she get?

$9 + x \leq 15$
$-9 \quad -9$
$x \leq 6$

Millie can get no more than 6 gallons.

Timothy walked 800 fewer steps than he walked the previous day. His fitness tracker battery died before he got home. He knows that he had walked 5,380 steps before the tracker turned off. He continued to take more steps after he got home from school. About how many steps did he walk the previous day?

$x - 800 \geq 5380$
$+800 \quad +800$
$x \geq 6180$

Timothy walked at least 6,180 steps.

Answer Key

Page 69

NAME _____

Lesson 5.9 Solving Inequalities in the Real World

Write and solve an inequality for each scenario. Give the reasoning for the inequality used.

Erica has some colored pencils. She wants to divide all of the pencils equally among her 8 friends. She wants to give them fewer than 6 pencils each. How many pencils does she have?

$$\frac{p}{8} < 6$$
$$8 \cdot \frac{p}{8} < 6 \cdot 8$$
$$p < 48$$

Erica has fewer than 48 pencils.

Ray has 11 boxes of rocks in his rock collection. He knows that he has at least 132 rocks. How many rocks could be in each box if each box contains the same number of rocks?

$$11r \geq 132$$
$$\frac{11r}{11} \geq \frac{132}{11}$$
$$r \geq 12$$

Ray has at least 12 rocks in each box.

Lamar can eat 2,000 calories a day at most. He has eaten 980 calories so far. How many more calories can he eat today?

$$980 + x \leq 2000$$
$$\underline{-980 \qquad -980}$$
$$x \leq 1020$$

Lamar can eat at most 1,020 more calories.

Spectrum Critical Thinking for Math
Grade 6
Lesson 5.9
Solving Inequalities in the Real World
69

Page 70

NAME _____

Lesson 5.10 Variables in the Real World

Julie babysits for her neighbor. She charges $10 for each hour that she babysits. If she babysits for 3 hours, how much will she earn?

The amount that Julie is paid **depends** on the number of hours that she babysits. The variable that represents her pay is the **dependent** variable. The variable that represents the number of hours she worked is the **independent** variable.

E = babysitting earnings h = hours worked
$E = 10h$ $E = 10(3)$ $E = 30$
Julie earned $30.

Write an equation or inequality for each scenario. Identify the dependent and independent variables. Solve the equation or inequality.

Wendy is saving money in her new savings account. She saves $20 a month. After how many months will she have $180 saved?

m = # of months (independent) $\frac{20m}{20} = \frac{180}{20}$
s = $ of savings (dependent)
$20m = s$; $20m = 180$ $m = 9$

Wendy will have $180 after 9 months.

Tiffany has a goal to read at least 150 pages in a week. It's the last day of the week and she has read 138 pages. How many more pages does Tiffany need to read to meet or exceed her goal?

p = # of pages to read (independent)
t = total pages read (dependent) $138 + p \geq 150$
$138 + p \geq t$ $\underline{-138 \qquad -138}$
$138 + p \geq 150$ $p \geq 12$

Tiffany has to read at least 12 more pages.

Spectrum Critical Thinking for Math
Grade 6
Lesson 5.10
Variables in the Real World
70

Page 71

NAME _____

Lesson 5.10 Variables in the Real World

Write an equation or inequality for each scenario. Identify the dependent and independent variables. Solve the equation or inequality.

Gerald buys gum for himself and his two friends. How many pieces of gum did he buy if he and each of his friends get 7 pieces?

g = pieces of gum (independent)
p = # of pieces for each friend (dependent)
$$\frac{g}{3} = p \qquad\qquad \frac{g}{3} = 7$$
$$3 \cdot \frac{g}{3} = 7 \cdot 3$$
$$g = 21 \text{ pieces of gum}$$

Oranges are on sale at the fruit stand. Juanita bought a bag of oranges for $5.35. The sale price was $1.50 less than the regular price. What was the regular price?

r = regular price (independent) $r - 1.50 = s$
s = sales price (dependent) $r - 1.50 = 5.35$
                                        $\underline{+ 1.50 + 1.50}$
                                        $r = \$6.85$

Original price was $6.85.

Callie earns $8.50 an hour doing odd jobs for neighbors. Her neighbor can pay her at most $51 to do some work at her house. How many hours can Callie work?

h = hours worked (independent)
p = total pay (dependent)
                              $8.50h \leq p$
                              $\frac{8.50h}{8.50} \leq \frac{51}{8.50}$
                              $h \leq 6$

Callie can work at most 6 hours.

Spectrum Critical Thinking for Math
Grade 6
Lesson 5.10
Variables in the Real World
71

Page 72

NAME _____

💡 **Check What You Learned**

Expressions and Equations

CHAPTER 5 POSTTEST

1. Harrison's baseball team uses a phone tree when a game is cancelled. The team mom calls 2 players. Each of those players calls 2 players, and so on. How many players will be called during the 4th round of calls?

$$2 \cdot 2 \cdot 2 \cdot 2 = 16 \text{ called}$$

2. Evaluate the expression: $3(10 + 3) \div (8 + 5) + 6 \cdot 4^2$ $3(13) \div (13) + 6 \cdot 4^2$
$$3(13) \div 13 + 6 \cdot 16$$
$$39 \div 13 + 6 \cdot 16$$

3. Write each phrase as an algebraic expression:
$$3 + 96$$
a. m less than 4 $4 - m$ 99

b. b represents Briana's savings total before a deposit. She deposits $30 into her account. $b + 30$

c. The quotient of 7 and m $\frac{7}{m}$

d. h represents the number of hours that Eugene works. What is his pay if he makes $8.50 per hour? $8.50h$

4. Write an equivalent expression for:
$11(x + 4) = $ ___ $11x + 44$ ___
$10x - x + 4x = $ ___ $13x$ ___

5. What is the **10** in the expression $10 + x$? ___ constant ___

Spectrum Critical Thinking for Math
Grade 6
Chapter 5
Check What You Learned
72

Answer Key

Page 73

NAME _____

Check What You Learned

Expressions and Equations

6. Solve for j: $6 + j = 27$.

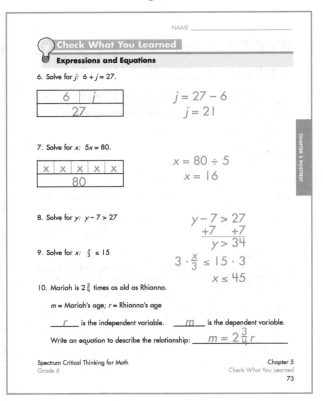

$j = 27 - 6$
$j = 21$

7. Solve for x: $5x = 80$.

$x = 80 \div 5$
$x = 16$

8. Solve for y: $y - 7 > 27$

$$\begin{array}{r} y - 7 > 27 \\ +7 \quad +7 \\ \hline y > 34 \end{array}$$

9. Solve for x: $\frac{x}{3} \le 15$

$3 \cdot \frac{x}{3} \le 15 \cdot 3$
$x \le 45$

10. Mariah is $2\frac{3}{4}$ times as old as Rhianna.

m = Mariah's age; r = Rhianna's age

___r___ is the independent variable. ___m___ is the dependent variable.

Write an equation to describe the relationship: ___$m = 2\frac{3}{4}r$___

Spectrum Critical Thinking for Math
Grade 6

Chapter 5
Check What You Learned
73

Page 74

NAME _____

CHAPTER 6 PRETEST

Check What You Know

Geometry

Find the area of each figure.

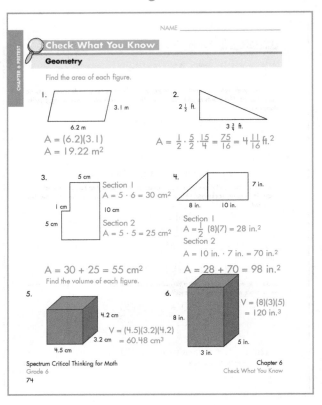

1.
3.1 m
6.2 m
A = (6.2)(3.1)
A = 19.22 m²

2.
$2\frac{1}{2}$ ft.
$3\frac{3}{4}$ ft.
$A = \frac{1}{2} \cdot \frac{5}{2} \cdot \frac{15}{4} = \frac{75}{16} = 4\frac{11}{16}$ ft.²

3.
5 cm
1 cm
10 cm
5 cm
Section 1
A = 5 · 6 = 30 cm²
Section 2
A = 5 · 5 = 25 cm²
A = 30 + 25 = 55 cm²

4.
7 in.
8 in. 10 in.
Section 1
A = $\frac{1}{2}$ (8)(7) = 28 in.²
Section 2
A = 10 in. · 7 in. = 70 in.²
A = 28 + 70 = 98 in.²

Find the volume of each figure.

5.
4.2 cm
3.2 cm
4.5 cm
V = (4.5)(3.2)(4.2)
= 60.48 cm³

6.
8 in.
5 in.
3 in.
V = (8)(3)(5)
= 120 in.³

Spectrum Critical Thinking for Math
Grade 6
74

Chapter 6
Check What You Know

Page 75

NAME _____

CHAPTER 6 PRETEST

Check What You Know

Geometry

7. Find the surface area of each figure.

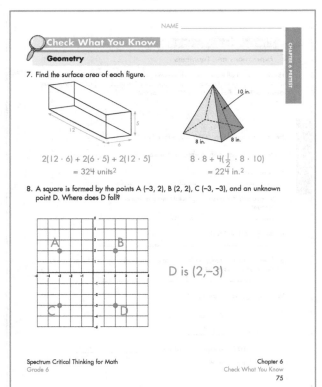

12
5
6
10 in.
8 in. 8 in.

2(12 · 6) + 2(6 · 5) + 2(12 · 5)
= 324 units²

8 · 8 + 4($\frac{1}{2}$ · 8 · 10)
= 224 in.²

8. A square is formed by the points A (−3, 2), B (2, 2), C (−3, −3), and an unknown point D. Where does D fall?

A   B
C   D

D is (2, −3)

Spectrum Critical Thinking for Math
Grade 6

Chapter 6
Check What You Know
75

Page 76

NAME _____

Lesson 6.1 Finding Dimensions of a Triangle

If the area of a triangle and one of its dimensions are known, the missing dimension can be found by solving an equation.

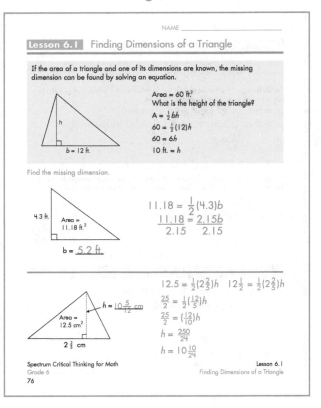

h
b = 12 ft.

Area = 60 ft.²
What is the height of the triangle?
A = $\frac{1}{2}$bh
60 = $\frac{1}{2}$(12)h
60 = 6h
10 ft. = h

Find the missing dimension.

4.3 ft.
Area = 11.18 ft.²

$11.18 = \frac{1}{2}(4.3)b$
$\frac{11.18}{2.15} = \frac{2.15b}{2.15}$
b = ___5.2 ft.___

h = $10\frac{5}{12}$ cm
Area = 12.5 cm²
$2\frac{2}{5}$ cm

$12.5 = \frac{1}{2}(2\frac{2}{5})h$ $12\frac{1}{2} = \frac{1}{2}(2\frac{2}{5})h$
$\frac{25}{2} = \frac{1}{2}(\frac{12}{5})h$
$\frac{25}{2} = (\frac{12}{10})h$
$h = \frac{250}{24}$
$h = 10\frac{10}{24}$

Spectrum Critical Thinking for Math
Grade 6
76

Lesson 6.1
Finding Dimensions of a Triangle

Answer Key

Page 77

Lesson 6.2 Finding the Area of Quadrilaterals

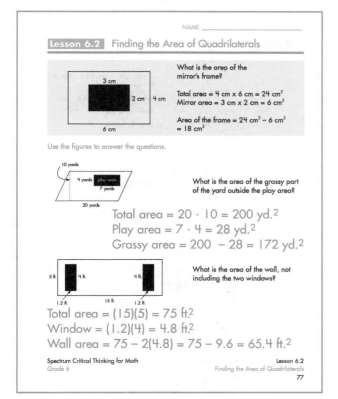

What is the area of the mirror's frame?

Total area = 4 cm x 6 cm = 24 cm²
Mirror area = 3 cm x 2 cm = 6 cm²

Area of the frame = 24 cm² – 6 cm²
= 18 cm²

Use the figures to answer the questions.

What is the area of the grassy part of the yard outside the play area?

Total area = 20 · 10 = 200 yd.²
Play area = 7 · 4 = 28 yd.²
Grassy area = 200 – 28 = 172 yd.²

What is the area of the wall, not including the two windows?

Total area = (15)(5) = 75 ft.²
Window = (1.2)(4) = 4.8 ft.²
Wall area = 75 – 2(4.8) = 75 – 9.6 = 65.4 ft.²

Page 78

Lesson 6.3 Finding the Area of Other Polygons

Find the area of each polygon.

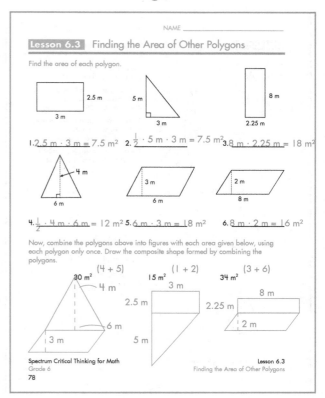

1. 2.5 m · 3 m = 7.5 m²   2. ½ · 5 m · 3 m = 7.5 m²   3. 8 m · 2.25 m = 18 m²

4. ½ · 4 m · 6 m = 12 m²   5. 6 m · 3 m = 18 m²   6. 8 m · 2 m = 16 m²

Now, combine the polygons above into figures with each area given below, using each polygon only once. Draw the composite shape formed by combining the polygons.

(4 + 5)   30 m²   (1 + 2)   15 m²   (3 + 6)   34 m²

Page 79

Lesson 6.4 Volume of Rectangular Solids

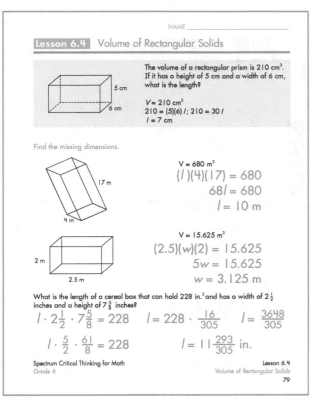

The volume of a rectangular prism is 210 cm³. If it has a height of 5 cm and a width of 6 cm, what is the length?

$V = 210 \text{ cm}^3$
$210 = (5)(6) l; \ 210 = 30 l$
$l = 7 \text{ cm}$

Find the missing dimensions.

$V = 680 \text{ m}^3$
$(l)(4)(17) = 680$
$68l = 680$
$l = 10 \text{ m}$

$V = 15.625 \text{ m}^3$
$(2.5)(w)(2) = 15.625$
$5w = 15.625$
$w = 3.125 \text{ m}$

What is the length of a cereal box that can hold 228 in.³ and has a width of $2\frac{1}{2}$ inches and a height of $7\frac{5}{8}$ inches?

$l \cdot 2\frac{1}{2} \cdot 7\frac{5}{8} = 228$ $l = 228 \cdot \frac{16}{305}$ $l = \frac{3648}{305}$

$l \cdot \frac{5}{2} \cdot \frac{61}{8} = 228$ $l = 11\frac{293}{305} \text{ in.}$

Page 80

Lesson 6.5 Using a Net to Find Surface Area

A **net** is a flattened-out 3-D shape. Find the area of each face, then add them together. The sum of the faces is the surface area of the shape.

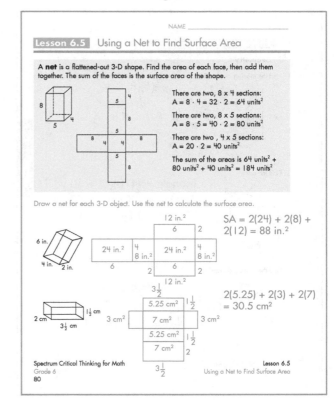

There are two, 8 x 4 sections:
A = 8 · 4 = 32 · 2 = 64 units²

There are two, 8 x 5 sections:
A = 8 · 5 = 40 · 2 = 80 units²

There are two, 4 x 5 sections:
A = 20 · 2 = 40 units²

The sum of the areas is 64 units² + 80 units² + 40 units² = 184 units²

Draw a net for each 3-D object. Use the net to calculate the surface area.

SA = 2(24) + 2(8) + 2(12) = 88 in.²

2(5.25) + 2(3) + 2(7) = 30.5 cm²

Answer Key

Page 81

Lesson 6.5 Using a Net to Find Surface Area

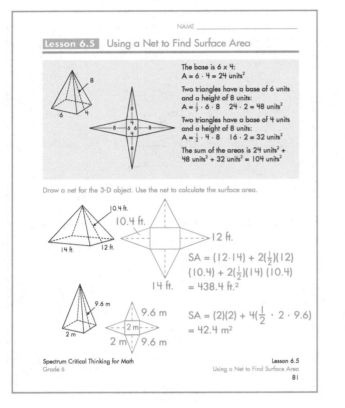

The base is 6 x 4:
$A = 6 \cdot 4 = 24$ units²

Two triangles have a base of 6 units and a height of 8 units:
$A = \frac{1}{2} \cdot 6 \cdot 8$ $24 \cdot 2 = 48$ units²

Two triangles have a base of 4 units and a height of 8 units:
$A = \frac{1}{2} \cdot 4 \cdot 8$ $16 \cdot 2 = 32$ units²

The sum of the areas is 24 units² + 48 units² + 32 units² = 104 units²

Draw a net for the 3-D object. Use the net to calculate the surface area.

$SA = (12 \cdot 14) + 2(\frac{1}{2})(12)$
$(10.4) + 2(\frac{1}{2})(14)(10.4)$
$= 438.4$ ft.²

$SA = (2)(2) + 4(\frac{1}{2} \cdot 2 \cdot 9.6)$
$= 42.4$ m²

Page 82

Lesson 6.6 Area on the Coordinate Plane

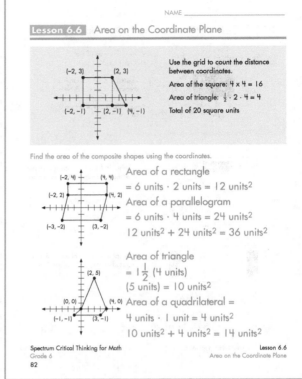

Use the grid to count the distance between coordinates.

Area of the square: 4 x 4 = 16

Area of triangle: $\frac{1}{2} \cdot 2 \cdot 4 = 4$

Total of 20 square units

Find the area of the composite shapes using the coordinates.

Area of a rectangle
$= 6$ units $\cdot 2$ units $= 12$ units²
Area of a parallelogram
$= 6$ units $\cdot 4$ units $= 24$ units²
12 units² + 24 units² = 36 units²

Area of triangle
$= 1\frac{1}{2}$ (4 units)
(5 units) = 10 units²
Area of a quadrilateral =
4 units $\cdot$ 1 unit = 4 units²
10 units² + 4 units² = 14 units²

Page 83

💡 **Check What You Learned**

Geometry

1. Find the missing dimension.

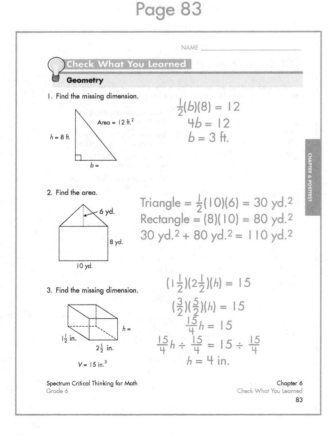

$\frac{1}{2}(b)(8) = 12$
$4b = 12$
$b = 3$ ft.

2. Find the area.

Triangle $= \frac{1}{2}(10)(6) = 30$ yd.²
Rectangle $= (8)(10) = 80$ yd.²
30 yd.² + 80 yd.² = 110 yd.²

3. Find the missing dimension.

$(1\frac{1}{2})(2\frac{1}{2})(h) = 15$
$(\frac{3}{2})(\frac{5}{2})(h) = 15$
$\frac{15}{4}h = 15$
$\frac{15}{4}h \div \frac{15}{4} = 15 \div \frac{15}{4}$
$h = 4$ in.

CHAPTER 6 POSTTEST

Page 84

💡 **Check What You Learned**

Geometry

CHAPTER 6 POSTTEST

4. Find the surface area.

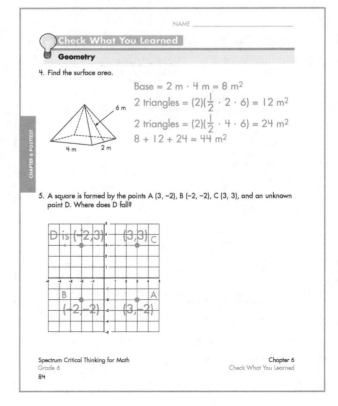

Base = 2 m $\cdot$ 4 m = 8 m²
2 triangles = $(2)(\frac{1}{2} \cdot 2 \cdot 6) = 12$ m²
2 triangles = $(2)(\frac{1}{2} \cdot 4 \cdot 6) = 24$ m²
8 + 12 + 24 = 44 m²

5. A square is formed by the points A (3, −2), B (−2, −2), C (3, 3), and an unknown point D. Where does D fall?

D is (−2, 3)

122

Answer Key

Page 85

NAME _____

Check What You Know

Probability and Statistics

CHAPTER 7 PRETEST

1. The ages of the 6 people taking a water aerobics class are 34, 66, 22, 55, 23, and 77.

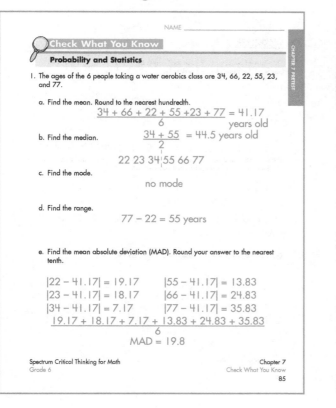

a. Find the mean. Round to the nearest hundredth.

$$\frac{34 + 66 + 22 + 55 + 23 + 77}{6} = 41.17 \text{ years old}$$

b. Find the median.

$$\frac{34 + 55}{2} = 44.5 \text{ years old}$$

22 23 34 | 55 66 77

c. Find the mode.

no mode

d. Find the range.

77 − 22 = 55 years

e. Find the mean absolute deviation (MAD). Round your answer to the nearest tenth.

|22 − 41.17| = 19.17	|55 − 41.17| = 13.83
|23 − 41.17| = 18.17	|66 − 41.17| = 24.83
|34 − 41.17| = 7.17	|77 − 41.17| = 35.83

$$\frac{19.17 + 18.17 + 7.17 + 13.83 + 24.83 + 35.83}{6}$$

MAD = 19.8

Spectrum Critical Thinking for Math
Grade 6

Chapter 7
Check What You Know
85

Page 86

NAME _____

CHAPTER 7 PRETEST

Check What You Know

Probability and Statistics

2. Create data displays for the data set at the top of the previous page.

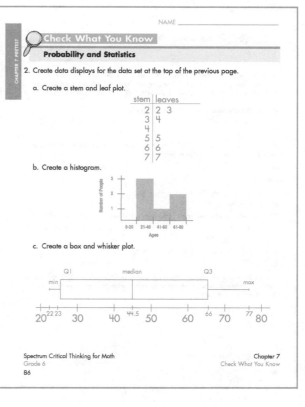

a. Create a stem and leaf plot.

stem	leaves
2	2 3
3	4
4	
5	5
6	6
7	7

b. Create a histogram.

c. Create a box and whisker plot.

Spectrum Critical Thinking for Math
Grade 6
86

Chapter 7
Check What You Know

Page 88

NAME _____

Lesson 7.1 Mean, Median, and Mode

Find the mean and median of each data set.

# of Letters in First Name				
3	8	8	4	10
3	3	9	3	7

First name:

Mean: 3 + 8 + 8 + 4 + 10 + 3 + 3 + 9 + 3 + 7 = 58

58 ÷ 10 = 5.8

Median: 3 3 3 3 4 | 7 8 8 9 10 $(4 + 7) \div 2 = \frac{11}{2} = 5.5$

# of Letters in Last Name				
5	7	5	6	5
5	11	20	9	9

Last name:

Mean: 5 + 7 + 5 + 6 + 5 + 5 + 11 + 20 + 9 + 9 = 82

82 ÷ 10 = 8.2

Median: 5 5 5 5 6 | 7 9 9 11 20 $(6 + 7) \div 2 = \frac{13}{2} = 6.5$

Is the mean or the median a better measure of center for last names? Explain your answer.

The median is a better measure of center. It is not influenced by the large outliers.

Spectrum Critical Thinking for Math
Grade 6
88

Lesson 7.1
Mean, Median, and Mode

Page 89

NAME _____

Lesson 7.2 Measures of Variability: Range and MAD

Measures of variability (including **range** and **mean absolute deviation**) describe how the values in a data set vary.

Calculate the range and mean absolute deviation of the height data.

6th Grade Students' Heights (inches): 79, 54, 51, 59, 63, 55, 59

79, 54, **51**, 59, 63, 55, 59
Range: 79 − 51 = 28 inches

|51 − 60| = 9	|54 − 60| = 6	|55 − 60| = 5
|59 − 60| = 1	|59 − 60| = 1	|63 − 60| = 3
|79 − 60| = 19		

$$MAD = \frac{(9 + 1 + 19 + 6 + 1 + 5 + 3)}{7} = 6.3$$

• Range is the difference between the largest and smallest values in the data set.
• To calculate mean absolute deviation, find the absolute value of the difference between the mean of the data set and each value in the set. Then, find the mean of the absolute values.

The closer the mean absolute deviation of a data set is to zero, the more consistent the set is.

The players on the basketball team are 65, 72, 67, 71, 73, 63, and 69 inches tall. Find the range and mean absolute deviation of the data set. Round your answers to the nearest hundredth. Range: 73 − 63 = 10

MAD   Mean: 65 + 72 + 67 + 71 + 73 + 63 + 69 = 480 ÷ 7 = 68.57

|65 − 68.57| = 3.57	|73 − 68.57| = 4.43	3.57 + 3.43 + 1.57 +
|72 − 68.57| = 3.43	|63 − 68.57| = 5.57	2.43 + 4.43 + 5.57 +
|67 − 68.57| = 1.57	|69 − 68.57| = 0.43	0.43 = 21.43
|71 − 68.57| = 2.43		21.43 ÷ 7 = 3.06

If a new player who is 85 inches tall joins the team, how will his height affect the range and mean absolute deviation of the data set?

It will increase the range from 10 to 22, and it will increase the MAD.

Spectrum Critical Thinking for Math
Grade 6
89

Lesson 7.2
Measures of Variability: Range and MAD

Answer Key

Page 90

Lesson 7.3 Analyzing Data in the Real World

Answer the questions. Show your work.

Jesse and Malik mow lawns to earn money for soccer uniforms. Last week, they mowed 7 lawns and made $168. The range of the amounts they were paid was $32. For 6 of the lawns, they were paid $19, $33, $27, $25, $34, and $28.

How much were Jesse and Malik paid for the 7th lawn?
$19 + 33 + 27 + 25 + 34 + 28 = 166$ Jesse and Malik were
$168 - 166 = 2$ paid $2 for the 7th lawn.

Find the mean and median of the data. Which measure gives you the most accurate picture of how the data is distributed?

Mean: $168 ÷ 7 = 24$ The mean is 24 and the
Median: 2 19 25 (27) 28 33 34   median is 27.

The median gives the most accurate picture. It is not influenced by the low outlier.

Find the mean absolute deviation of the data set. Which value is the outlier?

$|2 - 24| = 22$ $|25 - 24| = 1$ $22 + 5 + 9 + 3 + 1 + 10 + 4 = 54$
$|19 - 24| = 5$ $|34 - 24| = 10$ $54 ÷ 7 = 7.71$
$|33 - 24| = 9$ $|28 - 24| = 4$ MAD = 7.71
$|27 - 24| = 3$ $2 is the outlier.

The person who paid Jesse and Malik the least gave them an extra $20. What is the range of the new data set? How would the new number change the mean absolute deviation of the data set?

The range of the data set is $15.
The MAD would decrease.

Page 92

Lesson 7.4 Box Plots

The Carroll Cougars won 9 basketball games by 3, 2, 7, 15, 2, 4, 11, 1, and 6 points. Make a box plot for the data set.

Minimum = 1 Maximum = 15
1 2 2 3 4 6 7 11 15 Median = 4 Q^1 = 2 Q^3 = 9

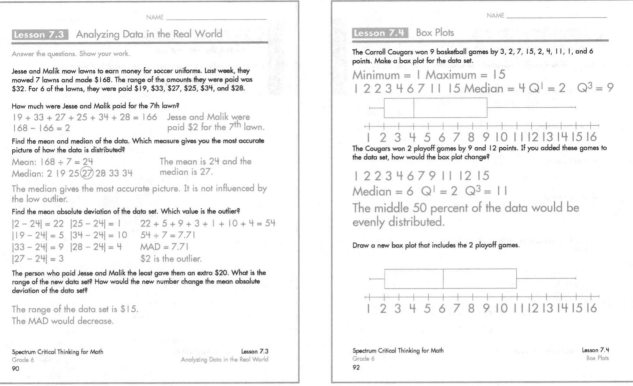

The Cougars won 2 playoff games by 9 and 12 points. If you added these games to the data set, how would the box plot change?

1 2 2 3 4 6 7 9 11 12 15
Median = 6 Q^1 = 2 Q^3 = 11
The middle 50 percent of the data would be evenly distributed.

Draw a new box plot that includes the 2 playoff games.

Page 93

Lesson 7.5 Stem and Leaf Plots

A data set can be organized into a **stem and leaf plot** by using place values. Each number in the set is converted to tens and ones. The tens digits are the stems and the ones digits are the leaves.

Make a stem and leaf plot to show the height data.
6th Grade Students' Heights (inches): 79, 54, 51, 59, 63, 55, 59

This allows you to easily see the minimum (51), the maximum (79), the range (28), and the median (59).

Stem	Leaves
5	1 4 5 9 9
6	3
7	9

Elian has scored 77, 82, 85, 75, 91, 85, 82, 89, 87, and 94 on his math tests this year. Draw a stem and leaf plot to show Elian's scores. Find the median and the range.

stem	leaves
7	5 7
8	2 2 5 5 7 9
9	1 4

Range: $94 - 75 = 19$
Median: 85

There is one more test on the last day of school, and it changes the mean of Elian's test scores to 86. What is Elian's final test score? What is the new range of the data?

Old mean: $75 + 77 + 82 + 82 + 85 + 85 + 87 + 89 + 91 + 94 = 847$ $847 ÷ 10 = 84.7$
New mean: 86 $86 × 11 = 946$ $946 - 847 = 99$
Final test score = 99
New range = $99 - 75 = 24$

Page 94

Lesson 7.6 Histograms

Histograms show the distribution of data by grouping data within a certain range and graphing the frequency of data points in the range.

Make a histogram to show the height data.

6th Grade Students' Heights (inches):
79, 54, 51, 59, 63, 55, 59

The histogram shows that most of the height values are grouped in the 50–59 range.

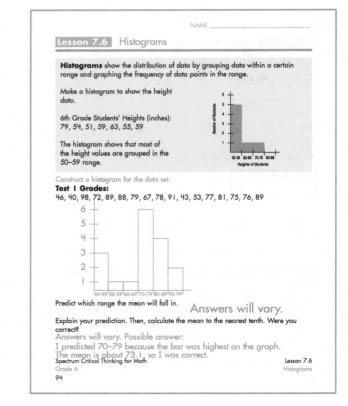

Construct a histogram for the data set.
Test 1 Grades:
46, 40, 98, 72, 89, 88, 79, 67, 78, 91, 43, 53, 77, 81, 75, 76, 89

Predict which range the mean will fall in.   Answers will vary.

Explain your prediction. Then, calculate the mean to the nearest tenth. Were you correct?
Answers will vary. Possible answer:
I predicted 70–79 because the bar was highest on the graph.
The mean is about 73.1, so I was correct.

Answer Key

Page 95

NAME _____

Check What You Learned

Probability and Statistics

The box plots below compare the amount of candy per bag for two brands of chocolate candy.

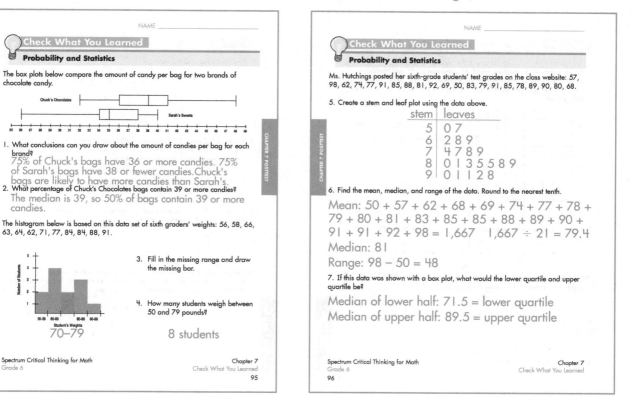

1. What conclusions can you draw about the amount of candies per bag for each brand?
   75% of Chuck's bags have 36 or more candies. 75% of Sarah's bags have 38 or fewer candies. Chuck's bags are likely to have more candies than Sarah's.

2. What percentage of Chuck's Chocolates bags contain 39 or more candies?
   The median is 39, so 50% of bags contain 39 or more candies.

The histogram below is based on this data set of sixth graders' weights: 56, 58, 66, 63, 64, 62, 71, 77, 84, 84, 88, 91.

3. Fill in the missing range and draw the missing bar.

4. How many students weigh between 50 and 79 pounds?

70–79

8 students

Page 96

NAME _____

Check What You Learned

Probability and Statistics

Ms. Hutchings posted her sixth-grade students' test grades on the class website: 57, 98, 62, 74, 77, 91, 85, 88, 81, 92, 69, 50, 83, 79, 91, 85, 78, 89, 90, 80, 68.

5. Create a stem and leaf plot using the data above.

stem	leaves
5	0 7
6	2 8 9
7	4 7 8 9
8	0 1 3 5 5 8 9
9	0 1 1 2 8

6. Find the mean, median, and range of the data. Round to the nearest tenth.

Mean: $50 + 57 + 62 + 68 + 69 + 74 + 77 + 78 + 79 + 80 + 81 + 83 + 85 + 85 + 88 + 89 + 90 + 91 + 91 + 92 + 98 = 1,667$ $1,667 \div 21 = 79.4$

Median: 81

Range: $98 - 50 = 48$

7. If this data was shown with a box plot, what would the lower quartile and upper quartile be?

Median of lower half: 71.5 = lower quartile

Median of upper half: 89.5 = upper quartile

Page 97

NAME _____

Final Test Chapters 1–7

1. Michael is shopping at the hardware store. He has $19. Does he have enough to buy 3 treated 2 x 4 lumber planks, 2.5 pounds of nails, and 1 can of wood stain?

Item	Price
Treated 2 x 4 lumber planks	$2.87
1 lb. of nails	$4.78
Can of wood stain	$7.77

$2.87 $4.78   8.61
x   3   x 2.5   11.95
8.61   2390   + 7.77
        956    $28.33
        $11.95

Michael doesn't have enough money.

2. William borrowed $1,014 from his grandparents to pay for his new laptop. He plans to give his grandparents $84 a month until he has paid back the full cost. How much will his last payment to his grandparents be?

```
    12
84)1014
   840
   174
   168
     6
```

The last payment will be $6.00.

3. Carpet is need to cover the room pictured below. The carpet costs $5.27 per square foot. How much will it cost to buy the carpet?

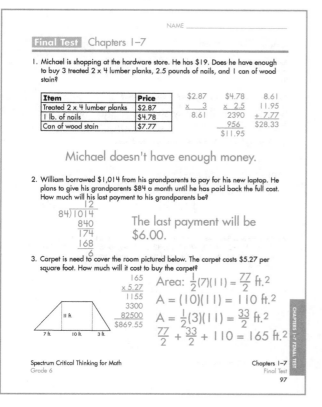

165
x 5.27
1155
3300
82500
$869.55

Area: $\frac{1}{2}(7)(11) = \frac{77}{2}$ ft.²

$A = (10)(11) = 110$ ft.²

$A = \frac{1}{2}(3)(11) = \frac{33}{2}$ ft.²

$\frac{77}{2} + \frac{33}{2} + 110 = 165$ ft.²

Page 98

NAME _____

Final Test Chapters 1–7

4. Carla ran $3\frac{1}{2}$ miles for every $2\frac{3}{4}$ miles that Skip ran. Complete the ratio table below.

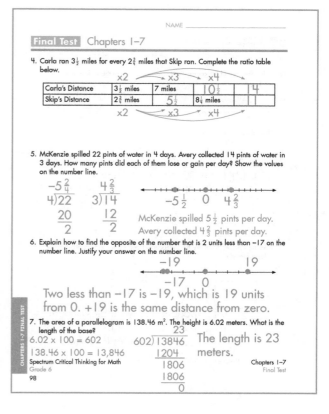

	x2	x3	x4
Carla's Distance	$3\frac{1}{2}$ miles	7 miles	$10\frac{1}{2}$	14
Skip's Distance	$2\frac{3}{4}$ miles	$5\frac{1}{2}$	$8\frac{1}{4}$ miles	11

5. McKenzie spilled 22 pints of water in 4 days. Avery collected 14 pints of water in 3 days. How many pints did each of them lose or gain per day? Show the values on the number line.

$-5\frac{2}{4}$ $4\frac{2}{3}$

```
   4)22    3)14
    20     12
     2      2
```

$-5\frac{1}{2}$ 0 $4\frac{2}{3}$

McKenzie spilled $5\frac{1}{2}$ pints per day.
Avery collected $4\frac{2}{3}$ pints per day.

6. Explain how to find the opposite of the number that is 2 units less than −17 on the number line. Justify your answer on the number line.

−19   19

−17   0

Two less than −17 is −19, which is 19 units from 0. +19 is the same distance from zero.

7. The area of a parallelogram is 138.46 m². The height is 6.02 meters. What is the length of the base?

$6.02 \times 100 = 602$

$138.46 \times 100 = 13,846$

```
        23
602)13846
    1204
    1806
    1806
       0
```

The length is 23 meters.

Page 99

Final Test Chapters 1–7

8. Jeff is tracking a helicopter in his area that includes Greenville (5, 3), Burlington (1, 1), Waysville (5, 1), Pilotsboro (3, 6), Denverson (0, 4), and Henderson (3, 2). The helicopter is currently at (–3, –4) and is moving quickly toward Greenville. Which town will it fly past the soonest? Plot the points and explain your answer.

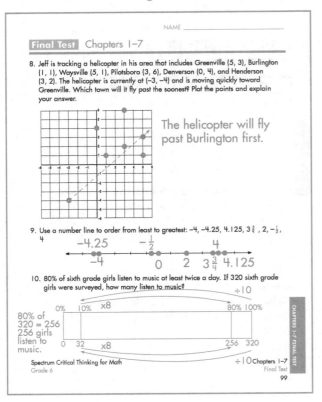

The helicopter will fly past Burlington first.

9. Use a number line to order from least to greatest: –4, –4.25, 4.125, $3\frac{3}{4}$, 2, $-\frac{1}{2}$, 4

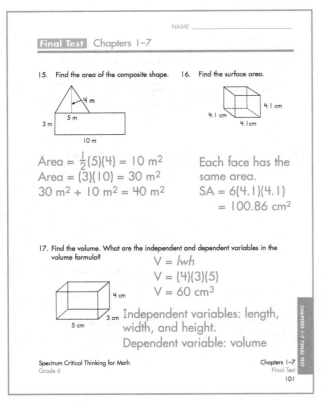

10. 80% of sixth grade girls listen to music at least twice a day. If 320 sixth grade girls were surveyed, how many listen to music?

80% of 320 = 256
256 girls listen to music.

Page 100

Final Test Chapters 1–7

11. Find the perimeter of the rectangle.

$(x + 2) + (x + 2) + (2x - 1) + (2x - 1)$
$(x + x + 2x + 2x) + (2 + 2 - 1 - 1)$
$6x + 2$

12. When the bell rang, 24 students were still in the cafeteria. 49 students had already left the cafeteria. Write and solve an equation to see how many students were in the cafeteria before the end of lunch.

$$x - 49 = 24$$
$$\underline{+49 \quad +49}$$
$$x = 73 \text{ students}$$

13. 9 dozen cookies can be made with $\frac{27}{2}$ cups of sugar. Write and solve an equation to see how many cups each dozen cookies needs.

$$\frac{9x}{9} = \frac{27}{2} \div 9$$
$$x = \frac{27}{2} \cdot \frac{1}{9} = \frac{27}{18} = 1\frac{1}{2} \text{ cups}$$

14. Amani is taking guitar lessons. She learns 2 songs with the hopes of learning at least 5 songs for the week. Write and solve an inequality that can be used to determine how many more songs she has to learn.

$$2 + x \geq 5$$
$$\underline{-2 \qquad -2}$$
$$x \geq 3$$

Page 101

Final Test Chapters 1–7

15. Find the area of the composite shape.

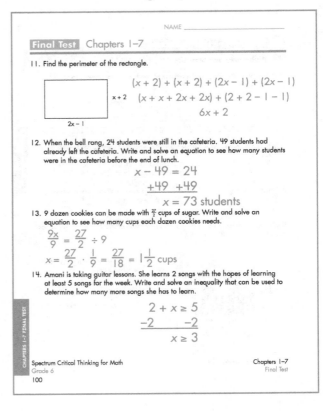

Area = $\frac{1}{2}(5)(4)$ = 10 m²
Area = (3)(10) = 30 m²
30 m² + 10 m² = 40 m²

16. Find the surface area.

Each face has the same area.
SA = 6(4.1)(4.1)
= 100.86 cm²

17. Find the volume. What are the independent and dependent variables in the volume formula?

$V = lwh$
$V = (4)(3)(5)$
$V = 60 \text{ cm}^3$

Independent variables: length, width, and height.
Dependent variable: volume

Page 102

Final Test Chapters 1–7

Jada is practicing for a big bicycle race. She keeps track of how many miles she rides each day. Here are the distances she rode last week: 14, 17, 1, 21, 19, 16, 41.

18. What is the best way to graph this data set? Why?

Box plot. It will clearly show extreme outliers and 50% of data distributed evenly around median.

19. Graph Jada's bicycle mileage using the method you chose.

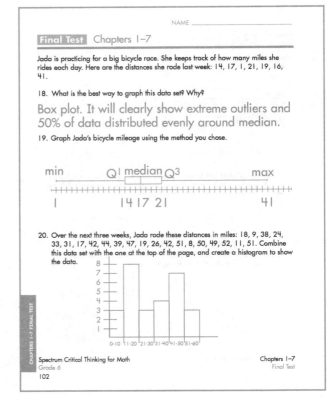

20. Over the next three weeks, Jada rode these distances in miles: 18, 9, 38, 24, 33, 31, 17, 42, 44, 39, 47, 19, 26, 42, 51, 8, 50, 49, 52, 11, 51. Combine this data set with the one at the top of the page, and create a histogram to show the data.

Notes

Notes